Shouting at the Telly

Rants and Raves about TV by Writers,
Comedians and Viewers

Edited by John Grindrod

faber and faber

First published in 2009
by Faber and Faber Limited
Bloomsbury House, 74–77 Great Russell Street,
London WC1B 3DA

Typeset by Faber and Faber
Printed in England by CPI Mackays, Chatham ME5 8TD

A CIP record for this book
is available from the British Library

ISBN 978–0–571–24802–5

2 4 6 8 10 9 7 5 3 1

For Mum and Dad, and for Carol – telly lovers all

Contents

Introduction

It's Time to Put on Make-Up, It's Time to Light the Lights . . .

What is the point of television, let alone a book about it?

Well, there is none, clearly. Glad we got that out of the way.

I'm not going to pretend that this book is for everyone. For a lot of people watching telly is a guilty indulgence they won't admit to, like Pot Noodles or masturbation (although if you can masturbate while eating a Pot Noodle I suspect that your pride in such manual dexterity would overcome any thoughts of shame). But they're not as bad as the people who think not having a television makes them Bono. This book isn't for them either.

It's for people who genuinely love watching TV: fans of long-running soaps, sitcoms, and dramas; people who follow the careers of quiz-show hosts, daytime presenters and celebrity chefs. From obsessives who hold grudges when favourite programmes are buggered about with, or can remember Penelope Keith's exact inflection in *The Good Life* when she says 'it's *not* good old Barbara, it is silly, *silly* Barbara', to the more casual viewer who enjoys stumbling across reruns of *The Apprentice* on Dave but couldn't give a toss about the story arc in *Buffy*. People with strong opinions about Fern Britton or Scott Bakula, *Lark Rise to Candleford* or *Blankety Blank*.

TV is a place where high and low culture mix. For that reason Proust would have made a great TV reviewer. He had three key attributes: firstly, he didn't get out much; secondly, he had a fondness for nostalgia; and, thirdly, an appreciation for how the trivial and the profound are inexorably linked. He might have done a list of Madeleine Moments, based around the rush he'd got from catching a glimpse of the rag doll from *Bagpuss*. A good TV review can throw a whole new light on what you've seen or articulate something you couldn't quite put your finger on. And that's what the contributors in this book aim to do. *Shouting at the Telly* might sound like a negative reaction to the TV, but I just like to think of it as people joining in, having a conversation with the programmes, expressing outrage or delight, rather than simply nodding off in the middle of *Heartbeat* and waking up with a bumpy and slightly sticky face where they've nuzzled and drooled on the remote.

There's no attempt here to be completist, balanced or objective: far from it, the contributors have written about whatever aspect of TV they liked, and as a result the pieces are hugely varied in tone as well as subject. But, my guess is, if you are a proper telly fan there will be more than a few sparks of recognition and the odd snort of indignation as you make your way through this book. I certainly won't ever think of *Howards' Way, Cash in the Attic* or *Goodnight Sweetheart* in the same way again. Behemoths like *EastEnders* and *Doctor Who* feel virginal, shiny and new as though they've been touched for the very first time. And some stuff even a grizzled old nerd like me had never heard of, but thank God for YouTube (I'm thinking specifically of Kevin Eldon's piece on *Supercar* here).

Ready for a bit of telly shouting? Thought so.

'You Bitch!' 'You Slag!':
The Sensitive World of Soap

In which Albert Square is demolished, specs fail to disguise sex, the Oil Baron's Ball causes a hoo-ha, Alan Dale takes over the world and Juhneen practises her evil hug face.

Ken Barlow is the most outrageous thing on television. William Roache has been playing Ken since the first episode of *Coronation Street* was broadcast in December 1960. How old were you then? I hadn't been born, wouldn't be for another ten years. A man has been constantly pretending to be another man to the entire country for ten years longer than I have been alive. I find this almost impossible to comprehend. Yes, people play characters in films and plays and TV series all the time who are *supposed* to be older than me. But on the whole they've been playing these characters for what, six months? A few years if it's a successful series. Not in real time for their *entire lives*. And they'd more than likely crop up in other things, playing other characters with different accents, hair or jobs, or find themselves recast mid-series or in some pointless 're-imagining'. Come Christmas 2009 William Roache will have been pretending to be the same made-up person continuously for forty-nine years. That's just not normal. Can there be anything of William Roache left inside there, cowering beneath the façade? And what if I die before Ken Barlow dies? Would that make Ken more real than I ever was? Are we all a figment of Ken Barlow's imagination? Is he in fact watching us, in some strange corduroy inversion of *The Truman Show*?

Deirdre is watching us, of that we can all be sure. Those glasses have to have some extra purpose. Okay, so she's lately traded her famous Hubble Space Telescopes in for some Sarah Palins, but I bet Blanche lets her have a lend of her mighty resin frames between takes, just so that Anne Kirkbride can stare deep into our souls and find us wanting. I could watch the three of them as a micro-soap all by themselves: Ken all concern and bluster; Deirdre ever cynical and salacious; Blanche increasingly crazed and merciless. The period after Tracy was banged up for murder was electrifying, with Ken and Deirdre caught in a spiral of recriminations and anger, and Blanche goading them on like some lugubrious imp. How disappointing to cut away to squeaky Ashley and moon-faced Claire when we could be watching three of the best actors on TV throwing their familiar old characters around in the acting equivalent of banger racing.

Coronation Street's strength has always been its ability to retain its cast. Sure, it messes up occasionally, losing an Anne Reid here or a Thelma Barlow there, but compared to the revolving door between Albert Square and whatever doomed musical is on in the West End that week, Corrie has maintained a core of long-running characters for decades: Ken and Deirdre Barlow. Jack Duckworth. Gail Platt. Blanche Hunt. Norris Cole. Audrey Roberts. Sally and Kevin Webster. Rita Sullivan. Betty Turpin. Emily Bishop. Given their stranglehold, it's almost impossible for new characters to make a mark, so it's brilliant seeing new people succeed. Becky Grainger, wonderfully played by Katherine Kelly, was such a slow burn that she was still to be seen in a former life in the ad breaks promoting cheese as her character slowly matured. Similarly, young David Platt has breathed new life into the rather moribund Gail and Audrey with a performance that sits somewhere between the Arctic Monkeys and Davros (Chavros, if you will).

If I find the idea of a fictional character walking around for longer than I've been alive a little odd (which it is, frankly; I'm not letting that one go), imagine moving into a soap set. Last autumn Brookside Close was sold at auction: the thirteen houses bought by Mersey Television in 1982 to house Phil Redmond's vision of suburban hell had been empty since the show's demise in 2003. Fancy moving into Brookside. Would you choose number five, blown up by a religious cult? Number seven, home of the siege? Number nine, scene of Laura's fatal electrocution? Number ten, with *that* patio. You'd feel like the new pre-packed soap family we've all seen arrive, misfire and leave without even a decent affair or a hastily introduced secret life. If it was down to me Brookside Close would be covered in an Eden Project-type dome and kept as a museum of the eighties, where everyone's either a lesbian, a murderer or a drug addict. But why stop there? The rent in Albion Market is more than reasonable, I hear. A ranch-style house in Knots Landing is the perfect location for anyone wishing to make glossy poolside pornos. And a timeshare in Los Barcos is probably a bargain. I bet Marcooth's villa is a snip, if a little lacking in atmosphere.

The Bitter End – Jim Shelley

How do I hate *EE*, let me count the ways. Answer: 8.7 million (approximately) – one for every viewer that watches it, making *EastEnders* (still) the most popular programme on British TV. Let's start, appropriately, with the most common – the ones that make me scream. Some of *EastEnders'* flaws are glaring, so embedded in the fabric of the show, they are well-known. Not that this makes them any better. In many ways, it makes them worse. No one on the show seems to be interested in addressing them.

The ethnic mix of characters in *EastEnders* is shocking. Always has been, always will presumably. Albert Square is so white, so patriotic and parochial, it's like watching a Party Political Broadcast by the British National Party.

Each year, the residents doggedly celebrate St George's Day. They set up a five-a-side team in memory of the '66 World Cup (which duly disappears after a week). They gather round the piano to re-create the spirit of the blackouts (not the kind Phil Mitchell has when he hits the vodka, the ones during the Blitz). Characters like Peggy Mitchell, Charlie Slater and Ian Beale are forever reminiscing about 'The Old Days' – when you could leave your back door open and the local bobby knew everyone's names (not surprising given that half the people in Albert Square are a bit dodgy, a bit moody, or as the rest of us call it, criminals). Chinese, Asian, or Caribbean families are still regarded as exotic (i.e. foreign), and come along as often as an eclipse. As for the idea of characters from as far away as Africa or the Middle East (or

France), they are unimaginable. It's only London after all;
the multi-cultural kaleidoscope that is the East End.

When they *are* allowed in, ethnic minorities have to
stick rigidly to their stereotypes. Patrick Trueman is forever drinking rum and dancing round his living room to
reggae, greeting everyone with the ostentatious cry of
'Yeh, mon!' The Masood family ran the Post Office and
then moved on to selling curry from a market stall. Their
children were (obviously) smart, decent and studious –
unlike all the white, English residents who are, almost
without exception, loud-mouthed, vulgar and thick.
Anyone not born and bred in Albert Square or London is
treated with extreme suspicion, especially if they're from
the North. Jason Dyer was a hard-line football hooligan,
a professional, violent thief, and a thug. Bianca's jailbird
boyfriend Whispering Tony King is a paedophile. Even
these are at a premium. Over twenty-three years, characters from Scotland, Wales or Northern Ireland have been
virtually non-existent. Like I said, it's only London.

The notion of Walford's residents travelling to cities in
Britain like Liverpool, Bristol, or Edinburgh would be on
a par with them paddling up the Amazon. In *Coronation
Street*, even über-chavs Les and Cilla Battersby have
made it to South Africa. The consternation with which
Ricky Butcher reacted to the news his dad was moving to
Manchester ('Manchester!?!') was recently repeated when
Lucas told Chelsea he was going to Leeds ('Leeds ?!?!') –
as if he was re-locating to Mars. But then in *EastEnders*,
even the rest of London is never mentioned. Suggesting
the residents might go to any of its famous parks, muse-
ums or landmarks would, obviously, be madness, but
they don't even know anyone who lives in another part

the sensitive world of soap

of town (or Britain). Middle-aged women like Ronnie Mitchell, Suzy or Tanya Branning don't have any friends who don't live on the square. The first two don't have any who do.

Virtually everyone except Max works in the market or on the Square – and what Max does for a living has never really been made clear beyond the fact that it allows him to splash his cash around and generally act flash. It's no wonder even the young characters treat going 'up West' as an act of extraordinary daring and decadence.

The producers still make great claims for the show's realism, not least when they crow-bar in storylines about issues such as bullying, knife crime or grooming. But whilst life in *EastEnders* is certainly humdrum (i.e., tedious), the outside world is a mystery. Barack Obama may bring peace to the Middle East before he gets a mention at the Slaters' kitchen table. They talk more about Bobby Moore than they do about Ronaldo in the Vic. They don't even watch *The X-Factor* or *Coronation Street*. Perhaps it's not surprising. Far from being your everyday, average group of families as they're supposed to be, the *EastEnders* are a peculiar bunch. Most of them haven't got a washing machine – forcing them to do all their dirty laundry (figuratively and literally) at Dot's launderette. When they want a cup of tea or coffee, they pay for it in Ian's grotty caff when they could just have one at home.

It's the minor gripes like these that make *EastEnders* so infuriating: Why, when anyone storms off or does a runner, do they always end up at the swings? Why do the local hard men (from Dirty Den to Mad Max) walk around at home in suits and shoes as if they were the

Krays, declaring their villainy by drinking scotch? In what way were we meant to believe that Stacey, the most savvy girl on the Square, would even go out with Bradley let alone marry him, let alone have a long, miserable affair with his father, Max? How do they afford these huge houses? Relatives, young and old alike, all live together in these Tardis-like houses as if serving a life sentence. Phil, for example, a man who despite being thick as shit owns several businesses, until recently lived with his mum in the pub – hardly ideal for an alcoholic.

Even when characters like Bradley and Stacey or Roxy and Sean get married, they hardly ever move out and when they do it's usually to somewhere that magically becomes available on the Square. The only thing that ever happens is the arrival of a long-lost relative turning up at the door – invariably someone who's never mentioned before. And we're not talking grand-daughters or cousins, it's usually bruvvers, muvvers, wives. Conversely, as soon as someone *leaves*, they are hardly ever referred to (or telephoned by) their remaining friends or family again.

These relatives will always be bad news – for a while. If they stay (like Jay, Jane Beale's brother Christian or Chelsea's father Lucas), they will eventually undergo total character transformation and be re-invented as All Right. But then character in EastEnders is a relative concept and fleeting. Petty criminals are harmless while the hardened variety (Phil Mitchell, Max Branning, Jason Dyer) are not really Bad at all – even when they're wielding shooters, doing dodgy deals, or beating people up with snooker cues. They have hearts of gold and they love their kids.

shouting at the telly

It's so laughable, it should be funny – not that you'll see anyone smile. One thing that has never changed about Walford. It's the most miserable place on TV.

12

Plain Jane Superbrain: When You're Hot, You're Not – James Donaghy

Slap bang in the golden age of *Neighbours*, a contemporary of Jason and Kylie, Des Clarke and Mike the mechanic, was Jane Harris, the most beautiful girl on television. Only no one told her she was the most beautiful girl on television because, well, that just wasn't what *Neighbours* had planned for her. For she was the ugly duckling who wasn't, the beauty that dare not speak her name and victim of the world's most redundant makeover.

Shipped off to grandmother Nell Mangel by her glamorous but cruel mother, Jane arrived at Erinsborough High with the unmistakable look of a lifelong victim. 'Do you know how many nicknames I've got?' she wailed. 'Heaps.' Damn straight. And none of them were flattering. Because Jane was Plain Jane Superbrain: the daggy, dorky, walking embodiment of how not to get down.

Neighbours needed to turn the nineteen-year-old goddess Annie Jones into an unattractive sixteen-year-old schoolgirl and the unique production values on which the show made its name were brought to bear on the project. Employing a bold minimalist approach they tied her hair back, stuck in some awkwardly placed hair grips and put her in large glasses.

Unfortunately, this just had the effect of making her even hotter than before. A thousand male fantasies were born as the palpably stunning Jones walked among schoolchildren looking like a fancy dress secretary. So we had the bizarre spectacle of every boy in the school

13

dismissing the supermodel in their presence as the dowdy geek queen of frump. 'Plain Jane Superbrain?? Don't make me SPEW! She's such a dag, mate! Who would want to pash with that?' Who indeed.

But the night of Plain Jane's unveiling was fast approaching. It was Prom night at Erinsborough High and Jane had managed to spawn a date with long-time crush Mike Young (Guy Pearce). Mike really saw Jane as more of a friend what with her not being sexually attractive (this bears repeating) so it was time for those two magicians of makeover Helen Daniels and Daphne the Stripper to go to town on the hideous Superbrain freak that was Jane Harris. As Helen Daniels presented the tarted-up prom queen in the Robinsons' living room, a slack-jawed Mike drooled like a retard at the vision of loveliness he had never fully noticed.

After that there was no stopping the no-longer-Plain Jane. She proceeded to date Mike for the next two years before he cheated on her and became Felicia Jollygoodfellow in *Priscilla: Queen of the Desert,* leaving Jane broken-hearted but wiser for the experience. There came further affirmation of her beauty when she was asked to become the first 'Lassiter's Girl', a modelling assignment where she would be the face of Erinsborough's weird faceless hotel complex that seemed to employ everyone at some point or other.

There was a strange coda to the Plain Jane saga. Her glamorous mother Amanda returned to Erinsborough and was so appalled that the daughter she raised as Plain Jane was now even hotter than her she immediately stripped her of her make-up, tied her hair back and forced those secretary glasses back on her. Don't call it a comeback but Plain Jane was back in effect. And yes, she was even sexier than before.

Jane's mum torment was not to last though as Amanda revealed she was on the run from the Feds on an insurance fraud rap and was just using Erinsborough as a hideout. The reverse makeover was all part of an elaborate cover story. Disgusted, Jane put her make-up back on and guess what? She was still hot. That's what happens with sexually attractive women. They are pretty much always hot.

Jane would finally find true love with Des Clarke. But being *Neighbours*, it could never last. Their engagement ended when Jane decided that nursing Nell Mangel back to health after a heart attack in England was a better bet than spending the rest of her life with the three-time loser Des. It was with a heavy heart that we bade farewell to Jane Harris. Her three years foxing around Erinsborough looking like Greta Scacchi will not be forgotten. Through her, we learnt the perils of gilding the lily, just how cruel schoolchildren can be and exactly how far detached from reality *Neighbours* liked to operate. We wouldn't have it any other way.

Ten Reasons to Love *Dallas* – Adrian Riches

The 1980s gave rise to a swathe of hit US prime-time soap operas that followed the lives of wealthy families and the big business that had helped make them rich. Amongst the most successful of these soaps were the high-camp *Dynasty* starring Joan Collins as super-bitch Alexis, *Falcon Crest*, which swapped oil for grapes, and *Knots Landing*, which followed the lives of four married couples in a Californian cul-de-sac. *Dynasty* may have given us that famous catfight between Alexis and Krystle and spawned insane spin-off series *The Colbys* with its incredible UFO storyline, but it's the less glamorous *Dallas* with the homely Miss Ellie and Southfork's kidney-shaped swimming pool that wins my vote. Here are ten reasons why . . .

The Opening Titles

With a title sequence that owed more to cinema than television, viewers were treated to panoramic views of downtown Dallas before the cast was revealed in alphabetical order via a sequence of cheesy montage triptychs. From the moment I first heard the big brass sound of the theme tune I was hooked. Comparing these impressive opening credits with those from the UK's biggest soap at the time that featured the rooftops of a dreary Manchester suburb followed by a quick glimpse of a rain-soaked cat, it's no wonder that TV audiences stared on agog at the overwhelming glamour. This title sequence had it all – it had cattle, it had oil, it had a shirtless Patrick Duffy and oh, a combine harvester thingy.

Sue Ellen Ewing

Played by Linda Gray and married twice to the series bad guy, the unscrupulous J. R. Ewing, former beauty queen Sue Ellen was a drunk and an unfit mother. Frequently packed off to the Fort Worth sanitarium, Sue Ellen would emerge, glass of bourbon in hand, with another plot to get back at the scheming J. R. When not drunk, under sedation or nipping down the shops to buy a baby she managed a string of affairs, but sadly none lasted longer than a bottle of cooking sherry for poor old Sue Ellen. Texas is a big state, which is just as well as no other soap could have provided enough room for her shoulder pads, never mind her hair. Inspiration for drag queens the world over, Sue Ellen was more Southend than Southfork, but at least she managed to make driving whilst drunk look glamorous.

Dodgy M & A Activity

There were no drawn-out negotiations or endless meetings with investment bankers for the oil tycoons of *Dallas*. Complex mergers and acquisitions were conducted in a single episode with companies changing hands quicker than a grubby fiver at the fairground. This is best demonstrated in episode 109, *Aftermath*, when Rebecca buys an oil company for character Cliff Barnes with the ease with which one would buy a toaster from Argos. Papers were drawn up (usually containing some dubious clause in the small print), signed by all parties and by midday it would be possible to take control of 51 per cent of Ewing Oil only to have sold it back to Westar by teatime.

There was something more than a bit naughty about Sly. Definitely popular with dads that watched the show, she became the best known of J. R.'s secretaries. Not happy with forty wpm, a Pret sandwich and some note-taking, Sly was a trusted confidante of J. R., at least when she wasn't spying on him for his bitter rival Cliff Barnes. She once temporarily headed up Ewing Oil before spending remaining episodes seated outside J. R.'s office wrestling with a typewriter cover. Her only respite was provided by attempts to fend off the occasional unwelcome visitor by shouting 'You can't go in there' whilst running for J. R.'s office door in five-inch patent heels. Sly also managed to get her boss locked up in the loony bin, which is probably not the best way to guarantee your Christmas bonus.

The Oil Barons' Ball

Providing us mere mortals with a glimpse into another more glamorous world, albeit one with oil rig-shaped ice sculptures, no episode of *Dallas* was complete without at least one mention of the Oil Barons' Ball. The main event in the soap's calendar except maybe for the Southfork barbeque, the ball provided the backdrop for some of the show's biggest dramas. The best being a huge fistfight between the Barnes and Ewing families in which J. R. throws a plate of food over Cliff Barnes who then bites J. R. The scene later provided a classic piece of dialogue when back at the ranch Sue Ellen asks J. R. 'How did he bite you?' to which J. R. replies, 'With his teeth.'

Pam Gets a Shock in the Shower

In one of the most mind-boggling storylines of all time Bobby Ewing played by Patrick Duffy returned to *Dallas* after being killed off at the end of the seventh season. Pam awakes on the morning after her wedding to some bloke called Mark only to find that he has disappeared. Pam wanders into the bathroom and a naked Bobby Ewing greets her as she reaches into the shower for the Head & Shoulders. Viewers were left wondering if Bobby Ewing had returned from the dead or if Duffy had reprised his role as *The Man from Atlantis* and stumbled into the shower whilst presumably looking for the sea. The whole mystery is solved (sort of) when it's revealed that Pam has simply woken up and it was all a dream. However, the question that most viewers were asking at the end of this implausible season-long dream sequence was why did Pam go to sleep with short hair and wake up with really long hair?

Lucy Ewing

Blonde, rich and with nothing better to do, Lucy (played by Charlene Tilton) charged about our screens in her silver Porsche earning herself the nickname 'The Poison Dwarf'. Ridden more times than a prize bull at the county rodeo and not exactly lucky in love, she managed to shag a chap who turns out to be her uncle before embarking on flings with the only gay man in Texas and numerous two-timing con men. Lucy's subsequent kidnap, rape, abortion and divorce pale into insignificance when compared to the true horror that was her big taffeta party frocks. A character so annoying that even her fiancée avoided her – preferring instead to remain in a coma.

The Krebbs

Despite being wealthy, Ray and Donna Krebbs lived in a house they'd built themselves at the bottom of J. R.'s garden. Somewhat reminiscent of a favourite auntie and uncle – you could be forgiven for thinking these characters had accidentally wound up in the wrong soap altogether. Donna always had more than a whiff of the Cheryl Baker about her, but despite never quite fitting in, she and her doting husband, dumb ole cowboy Ray, showed us a gentler side to Dallas life. At least that is until Ray pulled the plug on Mickey's life support and Donna's career success drove a wedge between the soap's nicest couple.

Who's Playing Miss Ellie This Week?

Lovable matriarch Eleanor 'Miss Ellie' Ewing was originally played by Hollywood star Barbara Bel Geddes, but in March 1983, Bel Geddes underwent a heart operation and missed filming for part of the season. Miss Ellie was temporarily written out and the next year, Bel Geddes stepped down from the role, but, bizarrely, rather than kill off the character, the soap's producers replaced Bel Geddes with actress Donna Reed. Later, with the show's ratings in steady decline, the producers reached an agreement with Bel Geddes and brought her back for the 1985–86 season leaving everybody confused, not least of all Bel Geddes, who appeared as though she'd wandered on to the set from a neighbouring old people's home.

Who Shot J. R.?

It was the cliffhanger that would go on to become the biggest water-cooler moment of the 1980s and guarantee huge worldwide audiences for the next season of the soap. It seemed as though just about everybody was speculating about who pulled the trigger and the storyline even made television news in the UK. Sue Ellen was framed for the attempted murder but it turned out that she couldn't have done it as she was probably in the sanitarium and eventually J. R.'s would-be assassin was revealed to be Kristen Shepard, his sister-in-law and mistress. With TV's biggest whodunit now solved audiences were once again able to get on with their lives and wonder what to do with their 'I shot J. R.' T-shirts.

Get Me Jim-From-*Neighbours*' Agent!
– Alex Young

The *Neighbours* cast has produced many noteworthy cultural icons. Where would pop be without Minogue, Donovan, Imbruglia, Vallance, McLachlan and, erm, Dennis? On the acting front, even the male least likely to graduate to the multiplex (no, not Bouncer, I'm talking Guy Pearce) has gone on to respected international film fame. But there is one ex-*Neighbours* star who's beaten them all, nearing the legendary 'six degrees' status of Kevin Bacon.

Yes, I speak of Jim-from-*Neighbours*. Actor Alan Dale has somehow contrived to be in nearly all of the water-cooler telly series of the past decade. Before we run down The Top Ten of Jim-from-*Neighbours* there are two questions to be asked: 1) Who exactly *is* his agent? Any of the current casts of *EastEnders*, *Emmerdale* and *Corrie* should get them on the phone and *beg* to be represented by them. And 2) Is it wrong that every time I see Alan Dale in anything, I *still* think, Ooh, hasn't Jim-from-*Neighbours* done well? Anyway, as Davina would say, Jim-from-*Neighbours*, here are your best bits:

Neighbours

A show stalwart for eight years; the nation mourned when Jim keeled over and had a fatal heart attack.

Lost

Jim appeared as powerful businessman Charles Widmore who decided penniless ex-monk Desmond really wasn't good enough to marry his daughter, leading to an ill-advised solo round-the-world trip by Desmond to try and prove his worth and much demented button-pressing on the mysterious *Lost* island.

24

Jim snagged a prestigious role as VP Jim Prescott, who in a major play for power votes to remove the President (David Palmer – the man whom Barack Obama has *totally* based his career on) 'temporarily' using the Twenty-fifth Amendment, whatever that is.

Ugly Betty

Jim portrayed another powerful businessman, Bradford Meade. You may be noticing a pattern emerging here, but then Jim does rock a suit and has a voice that drips gravitas. Bradford is quite the ladies' man, and gets lured into marrying gold-digging überbitch Wilhelmina Slater. Perhaps realising his potential error, he keels over and has a heart attack in the middle of the ceremony. This is becoming another signature Jim-from-*Neighbours* move.

The West Wing

Still in the Cabinet, but showing his versatility this time as Secretary of Commerce Mitch Bryce, Jim gets to ably support another heroically idealised liberal US President, Jed Bartlet.

The OC

This could be the *ultimate* Jim-from-*Neighbours* role, as grumpy business-and-ladies' man Caleb Nichol. In the noughties version of *Beverly Hills 90210* – or, at least it was until they resurrected the original – Jim again demonstrates that a) he's not good at choosing a decent, unselfish, totally-doesn't-care-about-the-money wife and b) he can do a dicky ticker. Narrowly escaping being poisoned by his cash-craving spouse Jim thwarts her and makes his exit courtesy of a fatal heart attack instead. It's going to be ironic if poor Alan ends up hit by a bus one of these days.

The X-Files

In a shock change from playing businessmen with grasping wives, Jim gets a three-episode gig as FBI agent 'Toothpick Man' in the final series. I'm not entirely convinced his character's nickname is as natty as the iconic Cigarette Smoking Man that he was created to replace. It lacks a certain 'hanging around in dark corners looking mysterious' élan. Despite, or for you conspiracy theorists out there, because of the fact that he was actually an alien, Toothpick Man managed to get access to the President (seen in a deleted scene), but it remains unclear what cabinet position Jim was aiming for at the time.

Torchwood

Jim once again displays his facility for being not-all-he-seems-at-first-sight as Professor Aaron Copley, Director of 'medical centre' The Pharm. Surely any institution that appears to be a trendy-sounding abbreviation of Damien Hirst's deeply awful nineties restaurant The Pharmacy *must* be engaged in nefarious deeds? Sure enough, the Prof is indeed up to no good, and ends up shot in the head by Captain Jack. But not before taking out the supernaturally pale and waxen-looking Owen.

Indiana Jones and the Kingdom of the Crystal Skull

A rare big screen outing for Jim. Manfully attired in uniform rather than his customary suits, Jim defends Indiana Jones against two FBI agents – those guys again, they just can't be trusted – as General Ross. Poor Indy has enough on his plate, having been nuked and blasted halfway across the desert in a fridge. Get the Feds off his case, Jim!

Heroes

Jim is revealed to be the CEO of the dastardly Company, who've been hell-bent on trapping, imprisoning and experimenting on the chosen few while also providing many foreign work jollies for horn-rimmed hunk Noah Bennet. After revealing his own power – he can mend hearts – Jim suddenly keels over, felled by the only heart he cannot heal: his own. The irony! Well, okay, I've made this one up, but as Jim's clearly somewhat of a cult legend, I'm holding this spot until Tim Kring decides he needs a superhuman of a certain age to add to his cast. God knows, with America's chronic obesity levels, Jim's would be the most potentially useful power any of them have exhibited thus far . . .

The Evil Hug Face – Mark Connorton

There are many skills necessary to be a good soap opera actor: you have to be able to pull a melodramatic face and then hold it for slightly too long while you wait for the closing theme music to kick in; you have to be able to cry and act drunk without making people want to point and laugh at you (though this is apparently optional for some people – I'm looking at you, Phil of *EastEnders*); and you have to be prepared for your character's personality to change radically in an instant, when you're required to suddenly turn gay for plot purposes, or to have a week-long booze-'n'-drugs downwards-shame-spiral. Most important of all, you have to master the Evil Hug Face.

Everyone knows what the Evil Hug Face is – it's when a no-good cheatin' spouse tells the cheatee that they love them and will always be there for them. They affectionately embrace, but then – gasp! – the cheatin' spouse makes a spiteful face over the oblivious spouse's shoulder, just in case anyone forgot what happened five minutes ago and needs to be reminded they are Up To No Good. It's slightly more subtle than the actor mouthing 'I'm lying, LOL!!!' and winking to the camera, but only just.

My favourite practitioner of the Evil Hug Face has to be Janine 'Juhneen' Butcher, *EastEnders*' most awesome bitch. Juhneen had a troubled and difficult childhood: she was brought up by such leathery horrors as Mike Reid, Babs Windsor and Pam St Clement; she kept disappearing for years on end for no good reason; and once she even mysteriously transformed into a swarthy Greek girl. When she returned as an adult (played by Charlie

Brookes) she had some fantastic plotlines (including the bit where she became hooked on coke, went on the game, and had to endure punter Ian Beale 'calling the shots' in some grisly bedroom scenario), but her height of awesomeness was when she seduced sad sack Barry Evans by holding a carton of curry up to his letter box and wafting vindaloo fumes into his hall.

For the next year or so, as Juhneen milked love-struck fool Barry for everything he owned, it was a non-stop cavalcade of Evil Hug Faces (combined with slight variations, such as the 'Ambivalent Hug Face' and the 'Actually I Feel A Bit Guilty Hug Face'). Whatever crucial plot point Juhneen had to convey through the medium of hugging and gurning, she nailed it; right up to the point when Barry tripped and fell down a hillside and Juhneen sat and watched him die while filing her nails ('If only he'd worn slip-on shoes,' she later cooed, upon returning from her honeymoon with the groom in a small urn). By the time she left the show, Charlie Brookes was so entranced by Juhneen's evilness that she ended every scene or garnished every hug with a random devious expression, whether or not the plot demanded it.

Other *'Enders* bad girls haven't really made the grade in the EHF stakes: Ian's Midwich Cuckoo daughter Lucy rarely bothers to hide her loathing and contempt for the pathetic earthlings she is trapped with, and sour-faced puffa jacket enthusiast Stacey has disappointingly turned out to have a heart of gold. Even when she was knobbing her fiancé's dad, she seemed to be more depressed than evil (which isn't surprising, as most of the knobbing took place in the gents' toilets in the Queen Vic). These days, if you want to see quality EHF action, you have to turn to cartoonish US drama series like *Desperate Housewives* or *Ugly Betty*, where camp old dames like Vanessa Williams and Nicolette Sheridan seem to spend half their screen time pouting smoulderingly over their co-stars' shoulders.

In the olden days, playwrights would give each main character a dull sidekick to discuss the plot with, or would have characters poncing round delivering soliloquies about what they were really thinking, but no one has time for that now (unless *EastEnders* is trying to be especially daring and has Dot Cotton delivering a thirty-minute Beckettian monologue about the absence of God over a nice cup of tea). These days, TV writers usually have to assume that viewers are kind of thick, so they can only get across a character's emotional states through the medium of really unsubtle acting.

Although it is incredibly cheesy, there is something pleasurable about spotting an EHF, just as there is with spotting other well-worn clichés – the fruit cart knocked over in a car chase, or the patient in a medical drama whose problems uncannily reflect the lives of the staff treating her. Despite its corniness and overuse, the EHF can sometimes work in a non-laughable fashion given the right actor and script. Don Draper, the studly protagonist of sixties-set advertising drama *Mad Men*, has been known to pull the odd EHF while embracing his Grace-Kelly-ish wife (and he has a lot to pull faces about, what with his two mistresses, fake identity and the fifteen tons of hair pomade plastered to his scalp), but Jon Hamm is such a subtle and restrained actor that it's more like a slight tightening of the eyebrows than a full-on EHF. It seems that as long as TV characters continue to lie to their loved ones, the EHF will be with us, and I wouldn't want it any other way. Embrace this proud dramatic tradition – and be sure to make a malicious face while you're doing it.

2

Sarah Beeny Thinks You're a Twat: Presenters and Factual Programmes

In which newsreaders parody themselves, property programmes find themselves gazumping each other, Bill Oddie
behaves like a total cult and home-shopping channels make
you lose the will to live.

I have a hot tip to beat the credit crunch, an idea to pitch
on *Dragon's Den*. Okay, so it's not going to pay off
immediately, but I reckon in twenty years I'll be a millionaire. It stems from *Supernanny*, where Jo Frost has
managed to popularise the use of naughty steps, corners,
mats and chairs around the world. My theory is that
when all these kids become adults there's an absolute
killing to be made from her discipline techniques – by
making fetish versions of them. No, really. I predict that
by 2029 Britain will see a boom in adult-sized latex
naughty corners or leather naughty steps, with domin-
atrixes dressed in tight Chanel suits telling their desperate victims that their behaviour is *unasseptable*.
Dragoness Deborah Meaden will love it, though she'll wait
for one of the other Dragons to say they'll invest half
before she expresses an interest, because that is her way.

Supernanny is, improbably, narrated by Nick Frost,
who's a good example for your kids to follow if you want
them to become zombie stoners or invade Paris in a tank.
When it comes to narration on factual programmes,

there's a definite hierarchy: if you hear football commentator Jonathan Pearce's voice on the telly chances are it's more likely to be half an hour of traffic cop mayhem and CCTV bloopers than the big match live; Samantha Bond, Sam West and Colin Salmon are at the top of the tree, their skill being the way they do not intrude upon the subject, and enhance the programme with their measured delivery. But there's also such a thing as getting carried away. Take Laurence Olivier in *The World at War*. Pretty straightforward gig for him, you'd have thought, and for the most part his delivery is beautifully soulful and effective. *I'm doing a telly, love,* he probably said to Joan Plowright as he marked up his script with characterful flourishes. *I know about war. I was Henry V, you know.* And he gets well into the part. He makes it his own. Perhaps too much so at times, because some of his pronunciation shows severe signs of over-thinking. Whenever Olivier has to say Ukraine he becomes Brett Anderson from Suede and we're treated to the strangulated whine of the great actor yelping *You-criiiiyne*. Similarly, when called upon to pronounce Stalin it sounds like Tara Palmer-Tomkinson doing a bad Sean Connery impersonation – *Shhtaaaah-leen*. And he says both of these things *a lot*. No doubt he was in the recording studio getting into the part as only a Shakespearian actor can, blacked-up and fencing in tights. For bizarre pronunciation he has been topped only by Gary Rhodes, who has lost his Estuary accent since the eighties and now has the peculiar mangled vowels of a French Canadian attempting a Dick van Dyke impression. A voice almost as unpleasant to listen to as the BBC1 announcer who sounds like he's much too excited about having a very blocked nose. You'll know him when you hear him. *Dis is BiBiSi Oned!*

Olivier's heritage passes directly to Kenneth Branagh in *Walking With Dinosaurs*. It's a slightly dodgy CGI-fest seemingly built around that one shot of the tyrannosaurus from *Jurassic Park* roaring into the rearview mirror of Jeff Goldblum's jeep, but with the added fun of hand puppets. Voice-over-wise you can see they were thinking gravity and authority to balance the visual absurdity, but boy does Branagh take that and run with it. And so what we're left with is not so much narration, more the lunatic ranting and cooing of Lear staggering around a blasted heath chatting shit about monsters, some of whom are his tiny muppety friends. Hear the tragedian's mighty bellow! I am at one with you, ankylosaurus and rhamphorhynchus, the last of my kind, the soon-to-be-extinct beast of stage, screen and gala awards ceremonies. I weep into my G&T, greasepaint running with tears, as the unhatched tyrannosaurus egg is caught up in the great cataclysm of a meteor strike. Oh noble creatures, I shall make you live once again! I shall make you *Roooooaaaaarrrrrr!*

Since 2000 lifestyle programming has eaten Channel 4's factual output. Phil, Kirstie, Gok, Gillian, Kim, Aggie, Kevin, The Beeny and that horrible witch from *Ten Years Younger* have acted like they're some government SWAT team, telling us we're too poor, frumpy, fat, dirty, clueless and old for the twenty-first century. Our shit smells, our pants are embarrassing, our wrinkles are ugly and our plans to better ourselves are risible. Will this zinc splashback really appeal to the young professional market? Are men really going to find these old leggings and Shakin'

Stevens stonewashed jeans attractive? Is eating pies really the answer? Their replies to these and other pressing modern dilemmas is a condescending and comprehensive no. We are all idiots. Bring on the experts.

Experts have a problem, though. They can be just a bit too, well, experty. And now their reign of terror has run for almost a decade their careers are all stuck in a bit of a rut. How we all cheered as Nicky Hambleton-Jones was ditched from *Ten Years Younger* for someone who actually was ten years younger. Gok, Trinny and Suzannah have all experimented with extraordinarily clunky brand extensions, getting swept up in their own makeover myth and ditching old favourites like *What Not To Wear* and *How To Look Good Naked* for a new collection of excruciating high-concept shows, dressing the nation or undressing wannabe models. The Beeny has seen the writing on the wall with regards to property development, and now her dating site is all over Facebook like John Barrowman on, well, everything. A glimpse into Kirstie Allsopp's ridiculous millionaire lifestyle in *Kirstie's Homemade Home* has made it obvious quite how far down her nose she must have been looking at those desperate scum on *Location, Location, Location*. But for the most part, their CVs are all looking a bit tired, and they don't want to end up like the woman who used to present *Home Front*. What woman who used to present *Home Front*? I hear you cry. Exactly. It wasn't always Lawrence and Diarmud duelling with their willies and ruining some poor bugger's house in the process, you know, but time moves on. What will our experts do next? What they really need is, well, an expert. Some bitter old HR exec to leaf her chipped nails through their tatty personal statements, shake her head and suck her teeth. So, Mr McCloud, you want a new prime-time TV show where rich people have to design a house of orgasmic perfection, called *If We Build It They Will Come*? Hmmm . . . Kim, Aggie – you want to front a natural history programme about the lack of hygiene in the animal kingdom, called *Nature Abhors a Vacuum*? I see . . . And you, Gillian, thinking of hosting a scatological gameshow where celebrities surprise their biggest supporters with their faeces, called *The Shit Hits the Fan*? Oh dear. Prepare yourselves for a condescending and comprehensive no.

Planet News – Rebecca Front

One of my first acting jobs was in a BBC comedy show called *The Day Today*, which was a satirical news spoof. What made it unusual was that the target of its satire was not the people who make it into the news – politicians, dictators, villains and the like – but the people who literally make the news – journalists. This suited me down to the ground. I am a news junkie; finding an English-language news channel is the first thing I do in any hotel room in the world – even before trying out the hand cream and checking out the tea- and coffee-making facilities. But I discovered early on that I had no aptitude for political satire and since I couldn't do impressions of either Margaret Thatcher or Cherie Blair, it didn't look likely that my obsessive news-watching would inform my career in any way. So when I was asked to play a variety of news reporters and presenters, all those hours of CNN and *Look South-by-South-West* came in handy.

Not that it took much research to come to the conclusion that most news presenters don't speak like normal people; they simply speak like other news presenters. It seemed as though there might be a school somewhere turning out people who paused before the last clause of every sentence, before finishing it off . . . with a swooping downward inflection. After a while, the content of their reports gets lost in the peculiarity of their delivery. It becomes as stylised as Noh theatre, a predictable opera of repeated cadences where meaning is no longer relevant, and pattern is all. There has to be a stentorian opening phrase: 'This may look like a quiet English town, but beneath the calm exterior, lies a dark secret.' Then a bit of heavy-handed sympathy for some hapless inter-viewee: 'How did you *feel* . . .? The whole package must then be neatly sewn up with some blindingly obvious word play: 'This is one pub in which Christmas spirit will come . . . in very short measures.' And lastly the all-important hand-back to the studio, always accompanied by a slight incline of the head: 'Back to you, Gavin.'

When *The Day Today* was first aired, a senior broad-caster self-deprecatingly suggested that it wouldn't be a bad idea to use the show as a media-studies training aid to stop journalists in the future falling into the same lazy habits. Well, more than a decade on, it looks as if this new generation has indeed been studying it closely. No longer do news journalists all sound like each other; now they all sound like our parody of them. Every clichéd inflection persists, but now even further removed from anything resembling real speech. Most mannered of all are those journalists who have reached the top of the tree and are allowed, as 'editors' in a particular field, to improvise their version of the day's events. The BBC's Martha Kearney, who happens to be a very natural com-municator, once said that she delivers these contextualis-ing mini-lectures as if explaining the story to her mother. This ensures that she clarifies enough for the uninitiated, but doesn't patronise her audience. If only others could find the same voice. All too often they appear to be addressing either some slightly drunk mates in the pub, or a highly-briefed parliamentary sub-committee. It's the middle ground that we viewers want – the context with-out the comedy routine, the facts without the stats. Above all, we want to be talked to in something approaching a normal, conversational style by people from the planet Earth, not . . . pause for gravitas, swooping downward inflection . . . from the planet News. And with a slight incline of the head, it's back to you, Gavin.

Cash In The Attic: An Editor's Disneyland
– Dan Maier

If you've never seen *Cash In the Attic*, congratulations on having a job. Ha ha, it's so easy to poke fun at the arid hinterland of daytime television, isn't it? To mock the creatively bankrupt expanse of cheap, bulk-produced programming, where Fogles and Sawalhas flit between hospitals, flimsily made-over houses and safari parks, interrupted only by commercials for debt consolidation or trailers for that evening's proper, professionally made programmes with a budget.

But look again.

There is much that daytime can teach us about how television is crafted. Well, all right, there's a bit that daytime can teach us. All right, there's one thing. That lesson is the art of editing. And our teacher is a programme in which members of the public flog their dusty tat.

Cash in the Attic sees a couple of experts comb someone's house for items of value. The McGuffin is that the householder has a particular low-rent dream that needs to be funded by the sale of said items at auction. It might be a holiday for an ill grandparent, a second-hand car for a university-bound daughter or a gold crack pipe for a kindly neighbour. Whatever it is, it is likely to cost around £1,000 and be entirely arbitrary. You can see the distaste on the faces of the participants as they're obliged to make out that the only way they can raise the money for a boating holiday on the Norfolk Broads is to flog a jewellery box and a few bits of furniture, when in reality they could afford it five times over without parting with so much as a brooch. But apparently there's no drama

39

without jeopardy, so just like *Time Team*'s misplaced belief that an archaeological dig is somehow more gripping if it's straitjacketed by a fatuous three-day time limit (whereas we'd actually be happy to see the dig last a month if it meant they actually found something other than some soil by the end of it), so in *Cash in the Attic* everything must hang on reaching the target. After deciding on the necessary sum and picking the items, it's off to the auction. And this is where the editor wields the power to create and destroy worlds. Almost.

As viewers have become more familiar with the machinery of television, so once-hidden roles such as that of the editor have become more visible. Reality show contestants now fret about how they'll be portrayed 'in the edit', while 'Making of . . .' programmes and the relative affordability of the means of production, in the form of camera and home-editing equipment, have contributed to a more telly-literate audience who now understand that what they see on the box is not necessarily the truth, the whole truth, nothing but the truth, or critically – RDF's infamous documentary about the Queen being the prime example – the truth *in the right order*.

So it is with *Cash in the Attic*.

What almost always happens at the auction is this. The first few items sell over their estimate, putting our householder ahead of target. This is going brilliantly! Two hundred quid for that watercolour? At this rate, they'll have literally to throw spending money into the canal to stop the narrowboat sinking. But then there's a twist. There'll be some trinket that the team are confident will provoke a bidding frenzy. But it won't reach its estimate and will go unsold. It's the toxic lot, somehow turning fate against our punter and triggering a run of unwanted items. The auctioneer will struggle. The bidders will remain unmoved. The items will go back in the cardboard boxes for the journey back home, where that painting will go right back over that light patch on the living room wall and that pewter cup will soon be refilled with pens and rubber bands in the kitchen. The dream is fading, the target disappearing, the barge sailing off into the sunset. Because, remember, they *absolutely can't afford to go on the holiday if they don't reach the target.* Even if they only fall a tenner short.

But of course it's always darkest before the dawn (you know, I'm not sure that can actually be right) and just in the nick of time, when all hope seems lost, the final lot will power through its estimate as it turns out that that soup tureen is an absolute must-have for two minted bidders with money to burn and a hunger to be seen on TV slightly raising their hand towards an auctioneer.

The target is reached, it's hugs all round and time to switch over for *Loose Women.*

So how come this is the pattern nearly every time? Do the programme makers place the items in the auction in the order they believe will yield the optimal dramatic flow? No. They just chop the auction to bits and rearrange the lots to suit their purposes. Continuity may be the editor's nemesis, but an auction, when you think about it, is his or her absolute dream, consisting as it does of a series of tiny narrative cells, all of which start (a lot is introduced) and end (the hammer falls) identically, meaning that like stretches of a child's train track, they can be rearranged and made to fit together in almost infinite ways, to create any narrative the makers want. You can shove all the successful lots together at the front and follow them with all the failures, creating a story of promise shattered by cruel failure. You can do it the other way round to present a fairytale of victory snatched from the jaws of defeat. You can mix them up and give yourself a narrative rollercoaster. All from the same actual auction. It's brilliant.

But there's one detail that gives this manipulation away. When introducing each item, the auctioneer, of course, announces the lot number. And this, as clearly as if the original footage bore a timecode in the corner, shows exactly what the editor's been up to. Just keep an ear out – the auctioneer will announce Lot 78 or some-such, and five minutes later will auction Lot 9. Many of these lot numbers are edited out of the final programme, but a few always remain. It might be laziness, lack of editing time or sheer barefaced cheek, but in any event, *Cash in the Attic* is lying to you and not even bothering to cover it up. It's a genuinely astonishing disregard not only for verisimilitude but for basic production standards.

Also, I really should get a job.

Repossession Repossession: The shows that launched a thousand insolvencies
– Susan Le Baigue

Once upon a time the main motivation for buying a house was that you needed a place to live. It was a home, a place where you'd be happy to stay at least as long as it took your family to outgrow it – although even outgrowing it didn't necessarily mean having to wave goodbye. When my parents had their loft converted in the mid-seventies it was because they needed the extra space but didn't want to move. Then suddenly people were having loft conversions to *add value*. No one owned a house, much less a home, we all owned *property* and *adding value* was the number one golden rule of *property* ownership.

I blame the telly. Well, a bit. Whilst clearly not as accountable as Dubya, coke-addled, bonus-crazed city boys and the whole sub-prime mortgage debacle in bringing about the current crisis in the property markets, I'd put money on there being at least a few people staring bankruptcy in the face who might never have been in that position had they not watched property programmes.

And it all started in the mid-nineties with *Changing Rooms*. The premise was simple. Flawed, but simple. Quite why anyone thought it a good idea to allow a neighbour to decorate one of their rooms without first having a chat about their likes and dislikes remains a mystery. Personally, I'd rather not let my next-door neighbour embark on making me a sandwich, much less totally gut and redecorate my spare room. But of course, it didn't take me long to realise that the series makers, and indeed the audience, lived for the inevitable design

43

faux pas. *So, is there anything you especially wouldn't want in your bedroom, Shirley?* Carol Smillie would ask. *Well, Carol, I hate purple and Simon loathes animal print,* Shirley would reply with feeling, before the action suddenly cuts to next door where Lawrence Llewellyn Bowen would be hanging purple leopard-print curtains with Shirley and Simon's neighbours (and soon-to-be former friends).

Something in *Changing Rooms* touched the hearts, or maybe the frontal lobes, of the nation's home owners and we were soon rushing en masse to Homebase and tarting up our places with a variety of dubious paint finishes and *themes* (I hold my hands up – I gave my kitchen walls a Mediterranean-style terracotta colour wash). And then, just as it became acceptable to turn the lounge of your tiny ex-local authority flat into a medieval baronial style hall, *The House Doctor* showed up.

Anne Maurice, with her giant dark glasses, high heels and sharp suits, was the Alexis Colby Carrington of the home revamp show. She swept down the garden path and into the lives of hapless individuals who were failing to sell their homes and explained, none too gently, why. Colour – *ugh*! Patterns – *seriously*? Pets – *they'll have to go*! Anything that smacked of the occupier having actually lived in their home was an absolute no-no. Potential buyers did not have the vision to see past a shag-pile carpet or a pink-walled bedroom. Anne Maurice de-cluttered, stripped down and painted over, ruthlessly turning every house into a magnolia-walled haven of bland tastefulness that would have prospective buyers salivating at the prospect of *putting their own stamp on it* (and thus, undoing all of Anne Maurice's work in a stroke).

And then Channel Four unleashed the two jewels in the property TV crown: *Location, Location, Location* and *Property Ladder*. It's funny that programmes based around the most expensive purchase that most people will ever undertake make for what must be some of the cheapest programming on the schedules. What should by rights be a twenty-minute programme is expanded to fill an hour with the not-so-deft use of the recap: *We're in Ealing, looking for a family house for Jenny and Tim. Outside space is important as is a large kitchen and space for Tim's extensive vinyl collection.* This is repeated after every commercial break plus clips from earlier in the show, and taken to extremes in *Revisited* shows, where the editor clearly believes we're suffering from collective Attention Deficit Disorder.

Maybe I'm bitter but I always found it hard not to hate the Jennys and Tims of this world, with their £600,000 budget in the country, the £350,000 for the crash pad in town and their inflated expectations. On one occasion Phil asked the prospective house-buyer what he thought of the view. He looked out of the window at the undulating green hills, the dappled sunlight, the expanse of blue sky. It was the very epitome of the bucolic idyll. In the very distance you could just about spy the gable end of another house. *Oh no*, he said gravely, *we really hoped not to have neighbours on top of us.*

Location set the bar for the property programme franchise, and, in their efforts not to appear to be shamelessly ripping off the format, every other property show to air since has had to include at least one entirely fatuous point of difference. In *To Buy or Not to Buy*, for example, the presenters (these two appear to be a dodgy used-car salesman and a nice-but-dim ex-public schoolboy) don't show the buyers around the house but instead leave them to their own devices while sitting in the garden (sorry, *outside space*), listening to the comments via a clunky-looking headset. There's absolutely no reason for this, other than it's different from how they do it on *Location, Location, Location*. In *Escape to the Country*, a show that first hit our screens hosted by Catherine Gee, a woman who appeared a little too much like Ben Fogle in drag for my liking, they took this to great lengths. *Escape*'s fatuous points of difference included:

Fatuous Point of Difference 1: What your budget would buy you elsewhere

The Escapees are shown a variety of jaw-droppingly gorgeous houses – a Jacobean manor in the Highlands or a rambling picture-perfect farmhouse with three acres in rural Lincolnshire, for example – all utterly pointless when the couple want to live in Hampshire where the same budget buys them a depressingly unloved 1970s semi with subsidence.

Fatuous Point of Difference 2: The Laptop Viewing

After whetting their appetites with the type of houses they haven't a hope of affording, Catherine leaves the Escapees and, in a breathtakingly pointless exercise goes off alone to view four properties while the Escapees watch, via the laptop, and are then permitted to choose just two of the four to view themselves. *Why?*

Fatuous Point of Difference 3: The Mystery House

Ah, the twist. Instead of picking two properties, the couple may choose to pick just one plus The Mystery House. Any viewer who's actually made it this far, and there can't be many, is silently pleading for The Mystery House. Otherwise in the second half we just watch the same houses we've seen in the first half with Catherine. And they don't get any more interesting the second time around.

Fatuous Point of Difference 4: Deal or No Deal?

It would appear the golden rule of *Escape to the Country* is that no one buys a house. Ever. After trudging dispiritedly around the two permitted houses, the Escapees try to appear vaguely enthusiastic whilst Catherine gamely attempts to persuade them to put in an offer. Sometimes she's really quite pushy about it, as though they are being unreasonable for perhaps wanting to look at more than two houses before making a life-changing decision. This never happens, as Catherine's closing voiceover reveals: *Barbara and Simon loved the Old Malthouse but decided against putting in an offer/are still waiting for a buyer for their own house/were pipped at the post by a higher offer/would rather drink battery acid.*

Escape to the Sun should be applauded for at least having a genuine point of difference: here the buyers viewed houses abroad, helping to drive prices across the Mediterranean and beyond out of the reach of locals. Actually, let's not applaud it after all.

The only UK-based property show that dared not to emulate *Location*, is perhaps the one with the most to answer for. *Property Ladder*. Sarah Beeny is the most bored-sounding person ever to front a TV programme but she has made a fortune in her work as a property developer, despite an apparent permanent state of pregnancy, and the programme soon convinced almost everyone else that property developing is easy money. The golden rule of *Property Ladder* is that no one must ever take this millionaire property developer's advice. Each week, Sarah's narration, delivered in a resigned monotone, breaks down the ignoring-of-advice into a specific list of where the would-be developer, let's call him Brian, is going wrong.

Where Brian is going wrong 1: Not budgeting properly

These people rarely have enough money to do the job they want to do but ingeniously get around the problem by simply not including everything in the budget. Brian blithely assumes that nothing will go wrong and everything will run to time and come in on (completely unrealistic) budget. Has he never seen the programme?

Where Brian is going wrong 2: The poorly thought-out development

Brian will almost certainly have come up with a plan that is overly complicated or just plain stupid, needlessly swapping the location of the bathroom and kitchen to ensure maximum re-plumbing, and coming up with some bizarre addition such as a games room adjoining the master bedroom. Sarah will advise him to ditch the games room and turn it into an en-suite, paying for it by keeping the existing bathroom where it is. But they'll have to agree to disagree on that one. Again.

Where Brian is going wrong 3: Not employing a project manager and/or professional tradespeople

Brian has had his head turned by the mind-boggling potential profit on offer and, with the grasping greed that so characterised the British property boom, wants to keep as much of it for himself as possible. To that end, despite having absolutely no experience, he has decided he will manage the project himself and do as much of the work as possible, including demolishing walls, digging up floors and – the ultimate sign of a man who has failed to recognise his limitations – plastering ceilings. All this whilst still holding down a full-time job. If, like me, you find it hard enough to muster the energy to do something as simple as boil a kettle when you get home from work, this is plainly madness and, sure enough, the project overruns by six months, Brian loses his job and, whilst ineptly going at a wall with a sledgehammer, he brings down all the ceilings, leading to the discovery that the joists are rotten. Thank heavens for the contingency budget. Oh, er, hang on . . .

Where Brian is going wrong 4: Becoming too personally involved

If you're doing up a house to sell on it needs to appeal to as many people as possible and wasting money on fripperies nobody wants is anathema to the experienced developer. Beeny can't emphasise this enough. But this doesn't stop Brian blowing the budget on a bespoke stained-glass window depicting Laurel and Hardy and a set of bathroom taps that cost slightly more than a BMW convertible.

49

Beeny's mood as she witnesses this wilful stupidity veers from mildly irritated to barely concealed fury. Brian, she repeatedly reminds the viewer, is doomed to failure. And yet, because this was still 2005, Brian invariably managed to turn in a handsome profit. And he will steadfastly refuse to take on board Sarah's explanation: it was a rising market and Brian could have made just as much money if he'd done nothing to the house and put it up for sale eight months on in the exact same state he'd bought it in.

But with rising markets a distant memory the Brians of the not-so-brave new property world are coming seriously unstuck, just like Sarah always said they would. It's probably a hollow victory for her though as it's hard to see how the hastily retitled *Property Snakes and Ladders* and its ilk will survive now. Perhaps I can reclaim several hours from the weekly TV schedules and everyone will stop looking at their house as an investment or a stepping stone to something bigger and better. Maybe it's time to actually enjoy it as a home, a place that you can have just as you want to without worrying about what Anne Maurice might think about your sofa.

Purple leopard print curtains anyone?

The Cult of . . . *Springwatch*? – Jim Helmore

Cult TV. Whether it's a groovy episode of *Adam Adamant Lives* or the terrifying 1980s BBC adaptation of *Day of the Triffids,* I love it. But what exactly is a cult show? I assumed it was something from long ago involving the strange or fantastic, watched by a handful of people at the time and remembered by even fewer now (*Goober and the Ghost Chasers* anyone?). Well, I did until the recent BBC 4 *Cult of* . . . documentaries about sixties, seventies and eighties TV were broadcast. The series started off with standard cult fare such as *Doomwatch* and *The Tripods* but then branched off into *The Brothers, Howards' Way* and eventually *All Creatures Great and Small.* This was all very confusing. And then, even more surprisingly, a new documentary nature programme came along that stretched my definition of cult even further.

Before I go on I must point out that I'm not a fanatical nature buff. I don't spend weekends in camouflage awaiting the annual migration of the lesser-spotted long-tailed tree-creeping warble tit. In fact, I go out of my way to avoid wildlife, particularly pigeons and our deranged local foxes. Therefore, all nature-based TV programmes, Attenborough included, I could take or leave – until *Springwatch.*

From the moment I saw it I was hooked. But I was also slightly worried. Give me a night in with *Spaced* or the *Clangers* and I know where I stand, but bat boxes, birds' nests and beetles? That's not natural, surely? It's been two years since I took my first tentative steps into this strange new world and now June can't come around quickly enough. I long for those precious evenings, sitting on the sofa with my hastily prepared dinner, my mobile phone switched off, a big smile on my face. I find myself 'telly-smiling', as a friend calls it, more and more as I get older: grinning inanely at an unfunny joke on *BBC Breakfast* or at the silly, scripted banter between Kirsty and Phil. It's embarrassing to catch myself telly-smiling, but doubly so if someone else sees me doing it. During *Springwatch* however, I telly-smile unashamedly.

Springwatch is a new breed of programme. With the head of a costume drama, the belly of a soap, the legs of a twelve-part thriller and the tail of *Big Brother*, where only mother nature gets to cast her eviction vote (her thumb turns down and a weasel is dispatched to wipe out a family of helpless chicks; she smiles and the hedgehog doesn't pick a would-be bonfire to hibernate in). Even better, *Springwatch* is proper live TV, where both you and the presenters never quite know what's going to happen next.

Oh yes, the presenters . . . Another reason to join the cult of *Springwatch*. First up, Simon King: an affable fellow, extremely knowledgeable and the most serious member of the ménage-à-trois. Then there's Kate Humble. She can soldier on bravely in the face of any animal mishap, talks to you as though you were eight years old and is also rather lovely (in fact, what ménage-à-trois would be complete without lovely, lovely Kate Humble?). And finally, currently taking a break from the show, there was Bill Oddie: the truly polarising member of the team. To some he was an irritating, hairy, open-shirted, grumpy-pants. And those people were probably right, but he was so much more than that. In this day and age, when television presenters are desperate to make a good impression, it was refreshing to find one who doesn't give a monkey's. Without Bill Oddie and his little strops, animal impressions and inappropriate jokes, can *Springwatch* survive?

The arrival of new boy Chris Packham seems to prove it can – his nightly 'spot the hidden Smiths song title' adds a whole new cult dimension to proceedings. But the programme's secret weapon is a wealth of genuine enthusiasm from *all* those involved, both in front of and behind the cameras. *Springwatch* exudes a love of nature that's highly infectious, encouraging us all to look out for the things that we would normally miss, ignore, or step on. And the show is hugely popular: its viewing figures would make even the most hard-hearted TV executive 'telly-smile'. The *Springwatch* message boards are jam-packed with questions and spottings and facts and footage. Even I, pigeon-loathing and bothered by foxes, have written about a nature programme and not *Doctor Who*. Could this be *Springwatch*'s biggest achievement yet?

With so many viewers and the fact that it's still in production, can *Springwatch* really be classed as a cult viewing? Perhaps a cult show is defined by the obsessiveness of its viewers, in which case I'm a card-carrying *Springwatch* fanboy and a cult programme it certainly is. Anyway, I don't have time to worry about that because the BBC has commissioned *Autumnwatch* to double my nature-nerd fix. Now all I need is a DVD box set with extras and commentaries.

Welcome to Knowsley: The Lost World of
Shopping Channels – James Bainbridge

A lot of television might be termed a 'guilty pleasure' – television that if we're honest we actually prefer to *Newsnight*; television that really we'd hope nobody caught us watching; television that deep down we know isn't good, isn't well made and yet is curiously watchable, addictive even. That isn't what I wish to discuss here.

For despite its poor production values and its curiously addictive qualities, despite the deep feelings of guilt I have in watching it – try as I might, it is hard to think of *Price Drop TV* as any kind of pleasure at all.

Let us be clear from the outset; I have never bought any product advertised on a home-shopping channel, I have never even been tempted – a fact which clearly does not account for the many hours, weeks, months I have lost absorbed in the particulars of sat-nav-clear-view-touch-screen-capability (I do not drive) or the handy lock-n-load-grassbox-no-clog-steel-blade-mow-n-go (I have no garden). I have not enjoyed this time. I can barely make excuses for it.

Heidegger felt that boredom was the pervasive mood of the modern age; deep, stultifying boredom in which all urge to pursue worldly concerns becomes subsumed by the preoccupation of the temper. This was an age in which the human need to be busy was alleviated by technology, and easy consumerism removed our purpose, bringing the objects of our desire straight to our door without any kind of strife.

At 3 a.m. sitting up in my dressing gown, watching a hand with obscenely painted fingernails – these fingernails actually have *pictures* on them – demonstrate the locking mechanism on a ten-foot storm-proof garden parasol; countering the urge to go to bed and sleep as I intended to five hours ago; listening to how this garden parasol, 'if you don't have a garden' (and surely that's me, surely this product meets my needs for shade despite my not having a garden), 'could be used at the beach, on a campsite maybe . . . or of course is ideal for use in the garden at home', is the last thing on earth that I would want to buy, and yet I can't stop watching it – it is easy in this moment to see what Heidegger meant.

Yet these channels aren't *creating* boredom, so much as representing it. This boredom exists independently within the world. It is what a lot of life is; but which television, too quick to amaze us with the remarkable – the wonders of the oceans as seen by David Attenborough, say – rarely properly represents. Television scarcely shows the absolute ordinariness of everyday human life. David Attenborough has never, for instance, produced *Life in Knowsley*, the painfully ordinary, perfectly boring borough in Merseyside.

'Welcome to Knowsley:' the road signs read, 'home of QVC'.

In fact, the signs have been altered in recent years – 'The future is K*now*sley', a knowing shift from *Sein* into *Zeit* – but QVC, Britain's first television shopping channel, remains there; a vast, grey, industrial shed. This kind of building has come to define the landscape of modern Britain: anonymously reproduced from a catalogue in every town across the country. *One Foot in the Past* would never have touched these buildings, yet if we are to look for a means by which to understand the modern predicament, we should turn to them; we should turn to the shopping channels as the best illustration of what we are about.

What shopping channels produce is televised boredom; it is ratings by incapacitation. It packages up the most insignificant subject matter – make-up brushes, batteries, multi-purpose remote controls – and presents them with such forceful enthusiasm – '*Seriously*, these air-tight resealable food boxes are going to *change the way you live your life*' – that it is impossible not to watch, it is impossible not to wait to find out quite how a lunch box will lead to a happier existence.

But let us not sneer, because this is actually skilled programme making. This ability to enthral over something as insignificant as a pleated curtain pelmet, or as gruesomely ugly as a six-inch crystal figurine of a car mechanic – 'ideal for Grandad, and remember, you can select the spanner in the colour of his birthstone' – is really quite an achievement.

They are easy to overlook, but these are surely the hardest-working presenters in television. They stand for hours on end in front of live cameras, talking constantly, thinking up new ways to sound enthusiastic about drill-bits, sandwich toasters and dolphin-heart eternity rings. Much like the plate-spinner at the circus, they create an alarming spectacle. They astonish in their ability to keep on speaking, but also induce a furtive hope in the viewer that something might go wrong; that any minute they might slip up, or drop something, or tell us what they really think.

It is day two of the Ideal World *Craft Weekender*; the Hay Festival of the quilling world. In the hierarchy of these channels – QVC at the top, their seductive soft-focus making electric carving knives look virtually pornographic; Price Drop TV at the bottom with its requisite shouting about bargains and throbbing graphics – the optimistically titled Ideal World sits comfortably in the middle. The woman on our screen, wide-eyed with fevered excitement, has been talking for five hours solid, the last hour in conversation with two middle-aged women from Birmingham – Kathy and Barbara, or 'The Glitter Girls' – about 'The Keepsake Bookafleur Cornucopia Set of Three Double-sided Boards'. Quite what this product is, this absurd jumble of disconnected words, is made no clearer by seeing it on the screen. For twenty-five minutes, immaculate fingers fiddle with these three fuchsia plastic tablets wrought with seemingly runic inscriptions with no explanation of what they're for other than:

'They're ideal to use with your set of eight Open Hearts *grande* peel-offs . . . If you were to say, Barbara, what's at the heart of what the Glitter Girls are about –'

'It would be the boards.'

'It would be the boards, wouldn't it?'

'That's what we're about. It's all about the boards.'

It's a shocking revelation that the Glitter Girls have nothing to do with glitter, but that's what they're about. It's all about selling the boards to the bored.

3

I Lost It with Bod:
Growing Up with Telly

In which a saggy old cloth cat reveals Stalinist tendencies, Debbie Harry's hair is beautiful, children across the land play at being Michael Grade and verbose American teenagers rock out on verandas.

Penfold was the best role Terry Scott ever had. Better than *Carry on Camping*, better than *Terry and June*, better than . . . Well, he must have done something else at some point. But, strangely for a cartoon, Penfold was the most three-dimensional character Scott ever played. *DangerMouse* was one of those children's programmes that was a little more sophisticated than it needed to be. Not just James Bond with rodents, the stories were more akin to a surreal *Two Ronnies* serial such as *The Phantom Raspberry Blower of Old London Town* than other children's programmes: washing machines took over the world in *The Day of the Suds*; a showbiz-crazed vampire duck brainwashed the Houses of Parliament in *The Return of Count Duckula*; Baron Greenback flooded the world with instant custard in, erm, *Custard*. And as with Susie Blake in *Victoria Wood As Seen on TV*, the uppity narrator frequently undermined the programme by slagging it off while on air, succumbing to delusions of grandeur.

A couple of years before *DangerMouse* my tiny mind was completely blown by something so sublimely odd that it made even talking turds *The Flumps* seem normal. *The Adventure Game* was a quirky little gem tucked away on BBC2 at teatime, where celebrities of an altogether more innocent age (the likes of Sue Cook, Liza Goddard and Fred Harris rather than their modern counterparts Jordan, Tara Palmer-Tomkinson and David Gest) arrive on the planet Arg, a kind of benign alien Guantanamo Bay, where Argonds, friendly alien dragons lead by a grumbling aspidistra and its eccentric butler, set them a series of intelligence tests and tasks to earn their right to go home again. Particular highlights would include watching seemingly intelligent presenters you'd looked up to for your entire childhood genuinely baffled by simple perspex mathematical puzzles, and the my-agent-is-going-to-pay-for-this look of panic induced by Australian Bill Homeward as he began speaking backwards to them. The programme would culminate in possibly the most exciting thing ever broadcast on TV – The Vortex. The celebs would have to navigate across a badly blue-screened grid while an invisible vortex of primitive BBC B-standard computer graphics, often guided by the players they'd lost along the way, attempted to evaporate them. Thus, pissed off loser Nerys Hughes would go after surviving team-member Derek Griffiths with the kind of ruthless determination usually only seen in Boba Fett from *Star Wars*. It was *The Crystal Maze* meets *I'm A Celebrity . . . Get Me Out of Here* with the production values of one of those *Doctor Who*s where they'd run out of budget.

Two particular female stars are worth mentioning here. The first is Lesley Judd, a hippyish *Blue Peter* presenter of such outstanding niceness that the programme makers used that gift and twisted it for their own ends. Judd became the 'mole' for a whole series of *The Adventure Game*, a not so innocent fourth celebrity who would join the team but be working for the Argonds, deliberately trying to make them lose the games and get evaporated. What a fucking bitch. And then there's Britain's Loveliest Lady, Moira Stuart, who, before she was a newsreader, played an Argond on *The Adventure Game*. This, together with her determination not to cry on camera during the boo-hoo fest that is *Who Do You Think You Are?*, makes her the coolest woman on telly by quite some margin.

My main childhood TV love was reserved for Oliver Postgate. Well, not the man himself, but the products of his wonderfully odd and beautiful imagination. Postgate set up Smallfilms with Peter Firminn, and together they created *The Clangers, Ivor the Engine, Noggin the Nog, Pogles Wood* and *Bagpuss*. It's his voice you hear on the narration, warm and slightly melancholy, as were the programmes themselves. If anyone is to blame for my TV addiction it is Oliver Postgate. The choc-o-late biscuit machine in *Bagpuss* (discovered to be a fraud perpetrated by mice) and Ivor rescuing sheep from the snow are far more vivid memories than, say, my first day at school. For me, the most preposterously brilliant of them all was *The Clangers*. You could be forgiven for mistaking this sad, absurd, dustbin-oriented series as a late work by Samuel Beckett. As Sir Michael Caine is wont to opine, in film acting, less is more. The range and subtlety of the performances Postgate got from these expressionless knitted toys voiced with a swanee whistle would shame the entire cast of *Hollyoaks*. No, that's too lukewarm a compliment. In fact, two of the most affecting pieces of acting I have ever seen on television come from the episode *Bags*, where the Clangers discover a lonely Gladstone bag who is drifting about in the celestial void around their moon, and by the end of the episode they have found a mate for him – a glamorous handbag – and the bags fly away together through space as the Clangers wave them off. Forget *Brief Encounter*, this is the greatest love story ever captured on film, and it's between two items of luggage.

A quick glance at *In the Night Garden* shows that children's programmes are as weird as ever. Various live-action and stop-frame creatures with ludicrous names such as Makka Pakka (with his og-pog, obviously) and the Tombliboos (who live in a bush) interact in the forest-like garden, with the sole aim, it would seem, of going to sleep. Thrillz. Amid this collision of *Teletubbies*, *Tweenies*, *Trumpton* and *Bagpuss*, the oddest thing of all are the Tittifers; a tree full of sinister hyper-realistic tropical birds all squawking away together, sending everyone to bed. How children sleep after seeing them I'll never know, but I predict we'll be seeing a lot of British horror films featuring tropical birds in the near future.

Why watching eighties *Top of the Pops* was about as good as it will ever get – Sam Delaney

Sure, there've been other shows. *The Simpsons* made me laugh. *The Sopranos* made me cry. And as for *The Dukes of Hazzard*, I look back now and realise that was nothing but a foolish infatuation. But I don't think anyone forgets their first true love – and mine was *Top of the Pops*. Can you really love a television programme? Yes, and *Top of the Pops* showed me how. How you could think about it day and night. How you could build your entire week around it. How you could go dry in the mouth and all of a quiver whenever it was in the same room as you. This was the early- to mid-eighties – the show's golden era, when it could draw audiences of more than twenty million. Punk was dead and a new generation of flamboyant, shamelessly poptastic chart acts came along to brighten the musical landscape. Each week, a random pairing of the show's brilliantly strange stable of hosts would preside over the action. The top acts in the world would swing by their White City studios to mime with gusto in front of an unfeasibly exuberant studio audience. And as this madcap carnival of pop unfolded, little squirts like me sat at home in open-mouthed awe, letting our Findus Crispy Pancakes go cold on our laps. We felt like we'd gained fleeting access to the greatest party ever thrown. Here are just some of the things that made it so special.

The Sneering Introduction

Something miserable like *Nationwide* had just finished. Suddenly, it was our special time. The posh-sounding continuity announcer could barely be bothered to hide his contempt as he said: 'And now on BBC One, it's time to learn about the latest developments in the pop charts from Jimmy Savile and Janice Long . . . it's *Top of the Pops.*'

'Shut it, Grandad!' I'd think to myself. 'The kids are taking over your precious BBC now, you crusty posh twat!'

The Opening Titles

And with that, the intergalactic sound of a disco-laser gun would blast from the TV's dusty speakers. Zzzeeeeeeooooow! It was the most exciting noise I'd ever heard in my life. TV screens spun through a cosmic vortex. Manic synth merged with frantic sax and galloping electro drums. A pink, seven-inch single with the words Top of the Pops emblazoned across it thundered towards my stupid face, then exploded into a million tiny pieces. 'Yee-ha! Everybody shut up, *Top of the Pops* is starting!'

The Presenters

'Hey hey!' shouted Jimmy Savile as an opening gambit. What kind of a way is that to introduce a prime time television show on the BBC? The *only* way! Forget today's earnest music presenters with their trendy haircuts and nerdish knowledge of Danish guitar bands. Savile was dressed in an ill-fitting white tracksuit and didn't have a flaming clue what the hell he was on about, much less a care. But did it matter? Not a jot. He wasn't there to bore us with details; he was there to whip us into a hysterical state of pop-fuelled dementia. And boy did he know how. As did the rest of that era's barmy and ridiculous menagerie of hosts. Janice Long in her jump suits; Bruno Brookes with his perm; Gary Davies wearing a white silk scarf like he was straight off down the Ritz with Pepsi and Shirley once the show ended. And let's not forget silly old Dave Lee Travis. I once saw him introduce a band while buzzing around the studio on a motorised monkey bike wearing a fireman's helmet. You can't plan that kind of televisual magic. It just happens.

The Set

We all remember the fluorescent tube lighting and the dry ice. But perhaps the sexiest aspect of that funky dungeon of pop was the raw, post-industrial styling. Think about it: in the real world, Mike 'Smithy' Smith would have just looked like some sort of spoddy Jehovah's Witness. But perched on a scaffold balcony clutching a skinny microphone he was somehow hot enough to marry Sarah Greene.

The Studio Audience

YouTube any *Top of the Pops* clip from 1983 and tell me Ecstasy only made it to these shores five years later. The BBC producers must have been putting something fishy in the fizzy pop because those youngsters, with their wedge hair-dos and dodgy jumpers, were having it big style, every single Thursday of the year. Their true moment of glory came during the presenter links when they would all crowd around in front of the camera, pouting and trying to cop a sly feel of Peter Powell's arse. Once, David 'Kid' Jensen thought it'd be fun to introduce Hot Chocolate by spontaneously shoving his mike in a young lady's mug and asking 'What d'you think of Hot Chocolate?'

'I can't stand them!' she responded instantly.

You should have seen the look on Errol Brown's face.

Boy George

'Give me time, to realise my crime,' sang George, all impertinent and sneering.

I blinked in amazement. Who in the hell was this? *What* was it?

'I'm sorry but I refuse to accept that she is a man,' said Mum.

'She is, Mum,' insisted my older brother. 'I read it in the *Mirror*.'

'Well,' said Mum, trying to draw a line under the discussion. 'If she is, then I think it's disgusting.'

Me, I kept my mouth shut and grinned at the madness of it all. Mum might not have got her head round it yet but I felt sure I had seen the future – and it was wearing dolly-pink blusher.

The Controversy

Adam and the Ants knife-fighting backstage! Frankie Goes To Hollywood being thrown out for lewd stage antics! George Cole and Dennis Waterman threatening to walk after the presenters failed to treat their Christmas hit 'What'll I Get for Christmas (for 'Er Indoors)?' with sufficient respect. Yes, even this brightest of shows had its darker moments. Perhaps none darker than the moment John Peel introduced Pete Wylie's 'Wah! Heat' by saying 'If this doesn't go to number one, I'll come round and break wind in your kitchen.' It's a wonder the licence fee managed to survive that one.

The Paraphernalia

Streamers, flags, T-shirts and even pom-poms – the stuff
those cavorting teenagers waved amidst that heaving
crowd seemed like precious treasure to my jealous eight-
year-old eyes. Then, one day, my brother reached the top
of their four-month audience waiting list. When I caught
a glimpse of him swaying to Spandau Ballet's 'True' I got
so excited I did a bit of wee in my jimmy-jams. When he
brought me home a plastic *TOTP* bowler hat I very nearly went one step further.

The Chart Countdown

Okay Mum, Dad, Uncle Arthur – you all know the rules.
If it's a song you like, you whoop. If it's a song you hate,
you boo. And if it's a song you either haven't heard of or
are just indifferent to, just say 'Hmmmm' and mutter
something non-committal. Ready? Okay, take it away
Simon Bates! *'At forty it's a chart entry for Starship with
"We Built This City".'* All together now: 'Yeeeeaaahhh!!!'

The Bands

Pop music is supposed to be fun. And not necessarily in
a Black Lace sort of a way. In the mid-eighties, every
band that passed through those *TOTP* studios seemed
conscious that they were there to help people at home
momentarily forget their worries. Some viewers had lost
their jobs. Some were striking miners. Others, like me,
had forgotten their PE kit that day and been forced to
play rounders in their pants and vest. Yep, life under the
yoke of Thatcherism was tough all right. But those
glittering pop-gods knew how to gently ease us through

67

it. Back then, pop stars were game for a laugh. Even Depeche Mode and The Cure could be cajoled into wearing Santa hats and having fake snowball fights on the Christmas episodes. As John Peel put it shortly before he died: 'It wasn't cool – because most people aren't cool. There was something attractively provincial about it. The fashions weren't hard-nosed and the dancing wasn't particularly good. If you watched it you wouldn't feel excluded. If you watched similar things now you'd think that unless you were fantastically good-looking, had huge tits and were prepared to wear virtually no clothing then you could barely exist as a human being.'

You're Watching STV – Steve Williams

Mike Read, draped from head to toe in tinsel, grins broadly and announces, 'Welcome to the Christmas *Top of the Pops*! We've got some great music coming up, starting with Diana Ross!' After a brief pause while she puts the record on, Diana Ross shimmies to 'Chain Reaction' in as lively a fashion as the tiny space between the radiogram and the dining table will allow, much to the delight of the audience of two people – well, apart from the one who's trying to decorate the Christmas tree and wants the tinsel back.

You probably didn't see that episode of *Top of the Pops*, unless you happened to be in our living room in 1986. I was Mike Read – I had to be, because I wore glasses – and my sister was showing off her meticulously choreographed dance routine.

Whether you presented *Swap Shop* in your bedroom or set up the *Krypton Factor* obstacle course in your back garden, almost everyone seems to have mounted their own versions of the TV hits of the day when they were growing up. In fact, one of my earliest memories is pretending to be Fred Harris, telling a story to a brick wall, in a rather primitive knock-off of *Play School*.

Initially my sister would be my loyal co-host in these endeavours – Sarah Greene to my Mike Read – but she soon tired of the egomania that demanded I always received top billing. Pretty soon, too, I found existing programmes far too constricting for my liking, and started creating my own formats. Soon, Studio 1 (my bedroom – my sister's room was Studio 2) became a hive of activity, producing hours of television, morning, noon and night.

My vehicles were, as you might expect from an eight-year-old, unbelievably derivative, mostly marathon Saturday-morning-style shows that spilled well into Saturday afternoons, with mine host reading things out of comics, talking about what he'd done during the week and, when it was time to have tea, introducing cartoons. Occasionally the shows would go on the road, being broadcast from such glamorous locations as my grandparents' back bedroom.

These lengthy shows gave me a level of exposure that even Jonathan Ross might think was excessive, but it never bothered my audience – helped by the fact my programmes were now broadcast to an audience of nobody except myself, as I always made sure my bedroom door was firmly shut and, preferably, my sister out at clarinet lessons before I launched into my introduction.

Eventually, of course, like all presenters, I hankered for more creative control and moved into production and management, setting up my own TV channel. A spare exercise book was turned into a listings magazine, as I painstakingly devised a week's worth of schedules for STV (well, naming your channel after yourself had worked for Lord Harlech). Broadcasting from 6 a.m. to 9 p.m. – because I went to bed at nine so had no interest in screening anything I wouldn't be able to watch – most days consisted of a breakfast show (presented by me), before schools programmes during the day, kids' shows (presented by me), then whatever BBC1 was showing around teatime before our prime-time variety spectacular (presented by me). Transmissions then concluded with an epilogue designed to send viewers to bed with happy thoughts . . . of me.

Management appealed to me, so much so that in the final years before puberty hit, I began to slim down my appearances in front of the 'camera' – though I still had a roving brief and kept the right to present any show should the fancy take me and my parents were safely out of earshot – and concentrated on my controller's job, putting together a killer schedule for STV. Programmes would be shamelessly nicked from other broadcasters – *Coronation Street* and *EastEnders* on the same channel at last! – and killer formats commissioned, as long as they appealed to our target audience. That audience, of course, mostly consisting of twelve-year-old boys from Wrexham with an obsession with comics, Phillip Schofield and Wet Wet Wet.

Sadly STV closed down shortly after, due to regulatory pressure, a lack of investment and its controller becoming more interested in spending time with girls than the *Radio Times*. Clearly, though, it was well before its time, as nowadays hundreds of TV channels seem to spring up every week, most with an even smaller audience than STV – who at least could sometimes count on its sister spying under the door to boost its ratings.

Life Lessons from Children's TV – Alex Young

When I was a child there was very little to do. Home computers hadn't been invented, neither had the world wide web, and no one wanted to virtually steal cars via games; they just got on and stole real ones. And even that didn't happen very often. If you wanted a toy to talk to you in the seventies you pretty much had to make up the voices yourself (incipient paranoid schizophrenia or creativity – who knows?). The most gobsmackingly exciting innovation when I was a girl was the Casio watch. So many buttons! What did all of them do? No idea, and anyway they were only really for boys.

In the absence of even such plastic exoticism as a My Little Pony, the seventies kid was left with TV. There were only three channels (and BBC2 only showed kids' programmes when there was dull old *sport* taking up BBC1 when *Blue Peter* should've been on) – the desperate parent of yore had to fall back on actually playing with their kids or inventing pointless things for them to do such as French knitting. Not for them the instant 'parent in a box' of CBeebies. Good lord, no. And even the meagre offerings that were available to ankle biters spent half their time showing you how to make Advent Crowns out of a pair of wire coathangers and some 'flame retardant tinsel' (um, that's *not a toy*) or telling you to 'turn off the television and go and do something more interesting instead'. What? No! I like watching telly! Give me more of that!

But at least the world of seventies children's TV prepared you for life as a grown-up and its many and varied challenges – not like all that loopy *Teletubbies* guff. Yes, the TV of four decades ago was instructional stuff – let's examine the evidence.

Bagpuss

Ah, Bagpuss, fat, furry catpuss. Owned by a permanently furious-looking small Victorian girl called Emily, Bagpuss was a kind of benign dictator. Emily was required to bring him a constant stream of 'things', and when Bagpuss got bored of them and went to sleep, all his friends had to go to sleep too. What? Couldn't Professor Yaffle carry on patronising people without Bagpuss? Couldn't Gabriel the Toad and Madeleine the Rag Doll go out and do a bit of busking, to supplement their meagre incomes? The Mice on the Mouse Organ surely hadn't done enough overtime to keep Charley Mouse in new trousers? No, dammit, once Bagpuss had finished his story, he was back to napping and the world had to grind to a halt. Clearly influenced by seventies unionism and the three-day week.

Life lessons from *Bagpuss*:

- Don't trust intellectuals – they're crabby, and they always try to ruin everyone's fun.
- Women, stay at home. And, er, take what you can get on the romance front – an ugly man who accompanies you nicely on a banjo might well be the gift horse whose mouth you shouldn't be looking in.
- Don't follow the example of startlingly young entrepreneur, Emily. She may have owned a prime piece of retail real estate, but it seemed likely she'd be hit hard by recession, rising rents and the like in the eighties, owing to the rather crucial fact that she *never seemed to sell anything*.

The Clangers

Strange, knitted creatures who lived on a knobbly little planet (described memorably by the narrator in one intro as being 'bleak and dull'. Jesus, we're kids! Couldn't you sugar-coat it a bit for us?) Despite even most small children knowing that the outer reaches of space are quite cold, the Clangers were attired only in some rudimentary armour as a top and what looked like flippers. Who were they expecting to be attacked by? If in fear for their lives, all they had to do was dive into one of their little burrows and clang shut the metal dustbin lid. And if you're going to be armoured, shouldn't your undercarriage be protected too? No logic, these yarn-based alien life forms.

The Clangers, communicating as they did in strangely melancholy whistles and toots, and not even really being able to chat that much to the Soup Dragon, seem to me now to embody the essential loneliness of life. For despite our modern cornucopia of central heating, telly chefs and Facebook, aren't we all really just living in burrows, eating Blue String Pudding and Green Soup and trying desperately to communicate with other people, whilst actually misunderstanding about 90 per cent of what they say? (Especially if you try to decode any of what the contestants on *The Apprentice* say to Surallan in the boardroom.)

Life Lessons from *The Clangers*:

- A 'directional' top and a lack of skirt or trousers, if worn for long enough, will render you impervious to the cold. *Useful for*: budding starlets and minor-league TV personalities looking to forge a career

through posing on red carpets in minimal amounts of clothing, regardless of the ambient temperature and wind-chill factor of Leicester Square in mid-February.
– You can live quite happily on soup. Well, we are in a recession.

Grange Hill

My mum wouldn't let me watch *Grange Hill*. Having viewed a few episodes, she thought it was likely to give me ideas about being what seemed, at the time, *extraordinarily* rude to authority figures. Thus, I was packed off to a draughty boarding school on the coast at the age of nine to not only a) miss out on all the important TV and films of the eighties, leaving me perpetually culturally bereft, but also b) to be raised by nuns. We were only allowed to watch *Tomorrow's World* (educational), *Top of the Pops* ('Surely none of those frilly-shirted and eye-liner-clad young men could activate any of our girls' nascent sexual feelings?' was, I'm sure, the logic there) and *The A-Team* ('Useful to know how to make a tank out of a Ford Fiesta and some old paint tins found in a garage you've been locked in, and also to work out how to sell an improbable idea to a large man who's a moron, week after week. If Sister Mary watches it with them, she can get some clues as to how to convince the girls Jesus was real, just by watching Mr T being endlessly duped. And she fancies Face a bit too.') So, to this day, I don't know how anyone survived being at a comprehensive (even the Grange Hill of the seventies seemed terrifyingly feral to such an undersocialised girl) and I doubtless missed out on many important lessons in How to Talk to Boys while I was at it. Damn you, Mum! (Later on, my mum wouldn't

75

let me watch *The Young Ones* either. Probably in case my head was filled with silly notions of going to university, being quite filthy, rebellious and political and owning talking hamsters. Kids these days would either demand a TV in their bedroom, or catch all this illicit action on YouTube or the BBC iPlayer. *That's* what I call progress.)

Life lessons from *Grange Hill*:

- Just say no. (Which I only gleaned from the *Grange Hill*'s appearance on *TOTP*.)

Keg-Parties, Ballads and Fake IDs – Angus Cargill

I should say at this point that, depending on your attitude toward US teen dramas, this piece may not be for you. If you're a person of taste and discernment you'll know that there are few greater things on television. I mean what more could you want from a drama than good-looking, verbose teenagers trying to figure out their lives and loves? And if you recognise this then you'll also be aware of the vital role that the soundtrack can play: from the illicit parties to the break-ups, the stolen kisses to the tragic accidents . . .

The Wonder Years

From a more innocent age, this show was always about nostalgia – from the heavy-handed voiceover to the period detail clothes – but while re-watching it on ITV3 now can be pretty tough, one thing that does stand up is its impeccable use of music, from its instantly recognisable and evocative theme tune (Joe Cocker's masterful take on the Beatles' 'With a Little Help from my Friends') to its featured tunes (Buffalo Springfield, Joni Mitchell etc.). In this sense the show was actually ahead of its time; just think of the CD tie-potential. And of course there was also the long-whispered, and sadly untrue, rumour that Kevin's sidekick Paul was played by a young Marilyn Manson.

My So Called Life

Unlike the above this had a terrible theme tune and was blighted by awful early-nineties incidental music, but in other ways this classic (that was discontinued after a single series that just happened to finish on the daddy of all cliff-hangers) helped define the conventions of teen drama music. Angela's heartthrob, Jordan Catalano, was the singer, song-writer and guitarist of wannabe band The Frozen Embryos (who become Residue after musical differences saw the original line-up split) and so was often seen plaintively strumming his guitar. They also pioneered the use of Indie-cred band cameos: one memorable episode saw Angela go to a club for the first time to see Buffalo Tom. They even had Juliana Hatfield, a hero of mine, I admit, in one of the final episodes, but perhaps the less said about that one the better (she played a homeless kid-cum-Christmas angel).

Dawson's Creek

Like *Friends*, this understood the need for a truly catchy (and, it has to be said, awful) theme tune, with Paula Cole's 'I Don't Want to Wait', and they pioneered the tie-in album, along with the books, the calendars, the pencil cases (sweating your assets, you could say).

The OC

While *Dawson's Creek* paved the way, it was *The OC* that really ramped things up a level. Producing six tie-in albums, when it only ran for four seasons, they had so much music to cram in that it often resembled one long glossy MTV music video. Who can forget their refrain-like use of 'Hallelujah' – first as Seth left to sail away into the sunset and later when Marissa died in a car crash – long before Simon Cowell got his mitts on the song. And in Seth, the character that just might have borne some resemblance to the show's creator, Josh Schwartz (or at least, how I imagine he liked to think of himself), they had the perfect indie kid: a comic obsessive with a neat line in self-deprecation and a large record collection. This show was also notable for having that other staple of the teen drama – the rock club, where various people drank (underage of course), made out and got into fights.

One Tree Hill

And so on to the greatest teen show of all time. Like the above-mentioned Seth, this also featured – in Peyton – a comic-book-loving (and drawing) teen with a wholly unbelievable, yet awesome, record collection. Alongside her ever-running webcam/blog her large bedroom was lined by retro vinyl bins, and to top it all she loved (in a non-ironic way) eighties metal alongside the emo bands of her day.

Now not all was musical peaches and pie – Haley's singing career for one thing was always hard to stomach (who came up with the idea of giving her and 'bad guy' Chris Ryan Adams' 'When the Stars Go Blue' to duet on? I think you'd struggle to find a song less suited to their voices), and the subsequent real-life crossover tour – but any show that manages to run Songs: Ohia's 'Just be Simple' and The Replacements' 'Here Comes a Regular' through its closing scenes is pretty inspired in my book.

This show also featured the required rock-star cameos aplenty – where else but Karen's small-town coffee shop would Sheryl Crow be wandering by at the exact point that Haley needed an emotional pick-me-up in Season

One – and an execrable theme tune from Gavin DeGraw. That said (and for some reason), when those piano chords kick in, my critical faculties always desert me and I'm ripe for some shameless emotional manipulation . . .

4

Doing a Telly:
The Dramatic Arts from *The A-Team* to *Z-Cars*

In which Gordon Jackson gets tongue-tied, we run along tower-block balconies in our rollers, have to sell The Barracuda, overcome oppression and are kept at the mercy of rubbish bosses.

When dermatologists, scarecrows or civil servants break into song and dance routines during otherwise dark and morally disturbing TV drama serials it can mean only one of two things: either you've leant on the remote during a Jimmy McGovern and ended up staring in dumb shock at *Britannia High*, or you're watching something by Dennis Potter.

Here was a man who knew exactly how to use telly to its best effect. Before *Pennies from Heaven* was broadcast in 1978 there really had been nothing else like it – a 1930s historical drama using songs from the era to tell a sophisticated adult tale of murder, rape and prostitution. It's not a musical in any conventional sense, as the characters only ever mime along with existing records, so they're more dream sequence than sung dialogue. Sheet music salesman Arthur (played by Bob Hoskins) yearns for life to be more like the songs he sells, and the gulf between the character's circumstances and the songs they are singing is horribly ironic.

The Singing Detective came next, and the 'Dem Bones'

sequence is one of the most memorable and breathtaking bits of television ever likely to be made, descending from a desperately humiliating hospital consultation to outrageous voodoo nurse-and-skeleton dance routine. Ewan MacGregor would never have had the chance to constantly get his willy out on the big screen if it hadn't been for his big break in *Lipstick on Your Collar*, jumping on a desk at the Foreign Office in a gold lamé jacket and miming along to 'Don't Be Cruel'. Because the title song from that drama is such a brilliant metaphor for the British invasion of Suez, which in itself is a perfect metaphor for the invasion of Iraq, *Lipstick on Your Collar* has remained particularly topical. There have been duff film remakes of *Brimstone and Treacle*, *Pennies from Heaven* and *The Singing Detective*, but they should be ignored in favour of the TV originals if you want to get a real idea of the genius of the man. In fact, until Pedro Almodovar, his natural heir in both style and theme, decides to remake a Dennis Potter script the cinema should leave well alone. Some things TV does better.

At the other end of the scale from Dennis Potter's extravagant set-pieces are Alan Bennett's *Talking Heads,* his two series of monologues. What could be funnier than Maggie Smith's vicar's wife Susan in *Bed Among the Lentils* describing how she rolled down the altar steps blind drunk from communion wine while flower arranging, or more heartbreaking than the end of her affair with Ramesh, the grocer, and her resignation to becoming a weapon in her oafish husband's assault on the Bishopric? There's a claustrophobic sense of doom and horror with which we watch Stephanie Cole's character Muriel in *Soldiering On* and Marjory, played by Julie Walters in

The Outside Dog, plunge blindly to their respective dooms like a couple of teenagers from a horror film.

The series is funny and unexpected, but it's also extremely dark and upsetting in places: Muriel's husband has abused their daughter, Marjory's husband is a serial killer, David Haig's park-keeper Wilfred goes to prison for paedophilia and Thora Hird dies twice. Yet Bennett finds strange and wonderful ways to save the two Patricia Routledge characters: a trip to prison for Irene in *A Lady of Letters* gives her the friends she's never had, and what amounts to prostitution to a foot fetishist in *Miss Fozzard Finds Her Feet* liberates another lonely old woman. On the whole, the first series, although bleak in parts, was a walk in the park compared to the cold and harsh second series, which was more like a walk in the park with Wilfred.

But, lest we forget, not all TV drama is a BAFTA-strewn orgy of genius. There's also *Rosemary and Thyme.* It's like the whole programme was spun-off from one of those ads for life insurance they show during *Countdown.* The title itself is an omen, but it's the stories that really stink: no tale is too stupidly contrived for our heroines to stumble across. It's a constant stream of babies under gooseberry bushes, mysteriously diseased plants and bodies buried in every bloody garden they ever dig up.

I know, I know: it's not even worth pointing it out, but the whole thing, it's just *preposterous*; a couple of middle-class gardeners stumble week after week upon intricate murder plots which they magically untangle, only to completely reset themselves at the end of every episode. Now, I'm used to suspending my disbelief when it comes to TV: I love *Primeval*, for Chrissakes. And telly is full of Jessica *Murder She Wrote* Fletchers and Henry *Pie in the Sky* Crabbes, solving crimes around their day jobs, but at least she's a crime writer and he's a policeman. I mean, Rosemary and Thyme really are just supposed to be a couple of menopausal gardeners. It leaves the way open for *anything* to be an ITV detective duo: how about *Lint and Fluff,* a couple of pieces of tumble-dryer fuzz who every week stumble across clues to a murder among the bits of paper left in the pockets of criminals who pass through a launderette. I'm thinking of wasting the time of James Bolam as Lint and Alison Steadman as Fluff. Or alternatively, I'll put my time into making up a detective series that actually, you know, makes sense.

When Lord Bellamy Looks at the Camera –
Andrew Collins

It is October 1971, a Sunday night. With its familiar fanfare, the LWT ribbon unfurls from left to right across a black screen. A simple title card reads *Upstairs, Downstairs*, under the imperious Alexander Faris theme tune (*dah-dah-da-dah-da-daah*); further captions inform us that the episode we are about to watch is called *On Trial*, written by Fay Weldon and set in November 1903 (this information is accompanied by suitable etchings from *Punch*). The establishing location shot: we pan across white-painted Victorian townhouses through a foreground horse and cart, as an upright gentleman in a top hat passes a furtive lady in long skirt and hat. She tentatively ascends the steps of 165 Eaton Place, a prospective parlourmaid. A butler impatiently redirects her to the servants' entrance, 'downstairs', thus deftly establishing in a wordless exchange the title's two-tier, olden-days caste system. A nanny with a pram passes across our field of vision, because it's television law. A portent of things to come, the downstairs bell rings before the maid has pulled the cord. Later, a bedroom light will go out before she has snuffed out the candle.

Inside, very much on a studio set now, we meet the staff, going about their subservient bustle: Mrs Bridges the huffing and puffing cook, Rose the snooty house parlourmaid, Roberts the crusty lady's maid, Alfred the Bible-spouting footman, Pearce the bottom-pinching coachman, Emily the dim-witted kitchen maid . . . the under-stairs hierarchy is quickly mapped out, with the poised and proper, permanently disapproving butler Mr

Hudson deferred to at all times. So it jars somewhat when Roberts addresses him as 'Mr Hudston' at the dinner table. While ladling out the mutton stew, Mr Hudson (which is his name), announces, 'Sarah is joining us as under-house parlourmaid, Miss Roberts.' She replies, clearly and confidently, 'Indeed, Mr Hudston,' adding, 'On trial, I take it?'

The maid may be on trial, but the actors, it seems, are not. Patsy Smart, who plays Roberts, hasn't learned her lines properly, has she? Even if she has, she still sloppily muffed the name of a principal character, in the first fifteen minutes of the first-ever episode of a brand-new series. I'm on the sofa, every time, shouting 'Cut!' and adding, 'Let's retake that from the top of page fourteen!' But they never do. I guess we should give Patsy a break: it's a big cast – lots of pesky names to remember – and the dinner-table scene is pretty complicated, with eight speaking parts and a lot of plate-passing; sufficient for the director to plough on regardless when one of his luvvies arses it up.

This is the cold, hard reality of a medium-budget ITV drama in 1971. The programme – which, to be fair to all concerned, began, unloved, in a graveyard slot and built its audience gradually – was shot like a stage play in the then-traditional manner, with fixed cameras, long takes and little time in a punishing turnaround for endless 'pick-ups'. Overdubbing would have been a luxury, hence the endless parade of misreads and muffs, the same kind they let Wilfrid Brambell get away with in *Steptoe & Son*.

Even Gordon Jackson, who, over five series and sixty episodes, made Angus Hudson (which is his name) one of TV's all-time great fictional creations, stumbles over his words and corrects himself, mid-sentence. In episode two, he demands, 'What has been going on bond . . . behind my back, Sarah?' And he's just described his master, Lord Bellamy, as the Undersecretary of State for something called the 'Admira*li*ty'. In the words of Mrs Bridges, it's a right two and eight and no mistake.

Lord Bellamy himself, played with upstanding dignity and humour throughout by David Langton, has a habit of looking at the camera. Well, not *exactly*, but he's constantly sort of glancing at it, especially when crossing the morning room for a sherry or to lean on the mantelpiece: he tries to ignore it while actually drawing attention to it. Langton honed his craft on the stage, you see.

Watching *Upstairs, Downstairs* makes me achingly nostalgic – not for the starched collars and shifting attitudes of the Edwardian era, but the two-inch tape glare and shifting sets of the 1970s, when period drama on television was still a case of erect chipboard, run up crinoline, block thesps, point camera and shoot. *Upstairs, Downstairs* may appear slipshod and not a little quaint to eyes more accustomed to the cinematic, location-heavy, deep-focus grandeur of *Cranford* or *Little Dorrit*, but what made it great was the storytelling, a skill that transcends the limitations of technicality. Ambitiously chronicling three decades of twentieth-century English life, dealing with shellshock, suicide, scandal, suffrage and the ultimate collapse of the old class system, its greatest achievement was to defy LWT drama controller Cyril Bennett, who said, 'It's very pretty, but it's just not commercial television. They'll switch off in their droves.' It went on to be shown in over seventy countries, and picked up two Baftas, seven Emmys, a Golden Globe and a Peabody.

Now I've revisited plenty of TV shows I adored in my youth and beyond that first Proustian rush, the majority really don't hold up. I may never again know the crushing sense of disappointment of buying *Starsky & Hutch* on video, or sitting excitedly down to a rerun on UKTV Drama of *Shoestring*, but *Upstairs, Downstairs* has survived, intact, as compulsive viewing. The goofs are all part of that. Just as they are affectionately logged on Steve Phillips's impeccable *UpDown* website, so they form part of the warp and weft of an epic series made before technology, especially digital, turned TV plays into a thing of the past. Now, even *Holby City* looks like a Hollywood movie. *Poirot*, still running after nineteen years, has lost much of its theatrical, drawing-room charm of late – it's all beguiling close-ups of his moustache or a daisy that add literally nothing to the unfolding plot, but might get the director his first movie job. In the words of Mrs Bridges: no good will come of it, you mark my words.

Let us, then, celebrate Patsy Smart for calling Mr Hudson 'Mr Hudston'. I have nothing but *admirality* for her.

Kill the Cops – Travis Elborough

George Orwell once wrote that it was usually in the most blissful circumstances – Sunday afternoons on the sofa, a belly full of roast dinner with a pipe of shag on the go – that the desire to read about murder took hold. While ascribing virtually criminal tendencies to the television itself in *Nineteen Eighty-Four*, Orwell didn't live to see poisoning, shooting, strangling and policemen, who not only carry revolvers but also use them with alacrity, become a mainstay of the small screen. The only gun smoke to found on Sunday afternoons for many years, however, stemmed from six-shooters carried by the likes of Lorne Greene. But Orwell's essential proposition that there was something intrinsically comforting to immerse oneself in the familiar tropes of violent death, deceit and detection remains as valid for TV as it was for literature. What's perhaps surprising is that we willingly go along with conventions in the genre that although tweaked and augmented from time to time remain . . . well, so conventional. I know this is how genre works. But really am I alone in wishing that a moratorium be held on the phrases 'I am taking you off this case', 'You've got forty-eight hours and not a minute longer' and 'The DA wants my butt'?

Why does no one in cop-TV land, for instance, ever say, 'I can see you've got quite worked up about this one, Jack; take as long as you like and don't worry about the rules.' Or 'Hang on to your badge; I know how important this thing is to your self-esteem, what with your drinking, the marriage break-up and the death of your daughter from drugs and everything . . .' Of course, it is the nature of the medium that if anyone did utter such words they would soon be taken up across the board and repeated elsewhere until equally ubiquitous. The cycles of innovation, proliferation and early Sunday night vehicles for John Nettles are notoriously rapacious in TV. Why, even the test card seemed to go in for shaky camera angles after *NYPD Blue* in the 1990s. Still we were all taking an awful lot of Ecstasy back then, I suppose.

From this box-set-fixated vantage point, and aided and abetted by that decade-shrinking wonder YouTube, it's the cravenness of it all that stands out. Like those stuffed crusts on pizzas, crime TV has largely survived by feeding us gimmicks that leave the main dish predominantly untouched. Every TV cop, after all, has had their shtick – even if that shtick was being a pathologist (*Quincy*) or wearing an unfeasibly lush and dark wig (*T J Hooker*) or not possessing a Y chromosome (*Cagney and Lacey*, *The Gentle Touch*, *Juliet Bravo*, *Prime Suspect*). Just as Conan Doyle gave Sherlock Holmes a cocaine habit to tie him in with the aesthetes, the choice of shtick is always cunningly bound up in the modes of the monde. It can be a fear of newly emerging microchip technology (*Shoestring*). Or, say, the misguided, if widespread, belief that living on an island with low taxation and an economy driven by service industries was a good thing (*Bergerac*). It doesn't really matter. In retrospect they all look like almost touchingly obvious attempts to ride whatever zeitgeist is going.

It is perhaps for this reason that certain tropes that were probably there present all along suddenly hove into view. Take the banging of fists on desks. Like power cuts and kipper ties, the sight of a DCI walloping a desk is intrinsically bound up in our idea of a 1970s cop show. Typically much show was made of it in *Life on Mars* – that occasionally smug, having-its-cake-and-eating-it exercise in patronising the recent past. When did it start, though? I have no idea. But I can't help harbouring a deep, if probably completely erroneous, suspicion that this particular motif couldn't have got under way much before the early 1960s.

This isn't because I believe that the gritty realism of kitchen-sink drama had somehow infected the police procedural form, or that shifting attitudes meant public displays of frustration were gaining more acceptance in this new Catch-Me-If-You-Can era of Benzedrine-popping teenagers than they once had. Though they probably were. And no doubt there are plenty of contradictory examples from the gung-ho shove-a-grapefruit-in-a-broad's-face days of noir. It's just hard to believe that the sets and/or the cameras would have coped with the pummelling bass beat of clenched dukes on plywood prior to that.

Watching vintage – and I use the word advisedly – black and white episodes of *Dixon of Dock Green*, the actors frequently seem far more sturdily wooden than any of the door-frames they cautiously squeeze themselves through. You suspect that the rigidity of the social types presented in the show (honest coppers, kindly old dears, aitch-dropping cockney burglars, weaselly turf accountants on the take, lithe young blondes led astray by would-be hoodlum boyfriends in turned-up jeans with Tony Curtis haircuts etc., etc.) didn't arise from any real desire to create a comforting vision of a stratified if collectively minded Britain where crime didn't pay and a game of ping pong could reform the meanest juvenile delinquent. No, they simply emerged out of a greater need to make life easier for BBC camera operators, carpenters and costumiers. This was crime drama from which the now perennial siege scene admonishment 'no sudden moves' could easily have stemmed. Even bicycles in heyday Dixon appeared restricted to mere wheeled-into-the station-lobby, walk-on parts.

But then Jack Warner's manor was a Queensberry rules kind of place; a TV-land version of suburban London where, outside of the ring, only cads and out-and-out wrong-uns raised their fists in anger. Here whistles, quiet words in ears and mugs of warm, sugary tea continued to be essential components in a crime-fighting arsenal.

Fast forward to the jump-cut-enabled film stock resplendent late sixties and seventies and TV's long arm of the law can finally go about devoting itself to pounding furniture (and occasionally suspects) and not just the beat. Dixon himself, by that time, was on his last legs. Struggling with potheads on his patch, he was finally given a desk job. Evidently mustering little enthusiasm for thumping it in the requisite fashion, he was soon found facing up to retirement.

Okay so, where there's a cop show there's a cliché, and, let's be honest, we obviously like it that way. And watching TV is killing time, which is infinitely better than killing ourselves or somebody else. Though I may well be moved to commit murder if I have to read yet another word on *The Wire*.

What *Howards' Way* Tells Us about the Eighties – Matthew Sweet

In the 1980s, the BBC was busily preparing for the possibility of nuclear war, selecting 78s for Radio 2 DJs to play from train carriages shunted to the least radioactive parts of Britain. It was a doomed policy: what they should have done was simply seal a series of *Howards' Way* in a lead-lined tin – because, once the human race had coughed its last, a new civilisation evolved from cockroaches would have been able to dig up one VHS box set with Maurice Colbourne and Jan Harvey on the cover – and deduce everything it might need to know about what the bombs had destroyed.

Howards' Way – it's important to get the apostrophe in the right place – was a watery, more entrepreneurial version of *The Brothers*, the road-haulage-related family saga of the Wilson years. It ran for six years, outlived its lead actor, developed the art of the nautical montage sequence with synth-pop-ballad soundtrack and gave Dulcie Gray something to do in the afternoons. But it also captured the spirit of its age – on glossy location 16 mm and videotaped studio scenes lit with all the subtlety of the *Breakfast Time* studio. *Howards' Way* was the 1980s.

Principally, the series was about people in pastel clothes having extra-marital affairs and debating the pros and cons of fibreglass boat design. Whole scenes could consist of someone giving a flipchart presentation about tank-testing a lightweight catamaran. However – and this was the joy of it – *Howards' Way* made the language of 1980s free enterprise sound as arcane and as meaningless as that of the starship *Enterprise*. Its characters – the business brains of a waterside town somewhere near Portsmouth – knitted their brows behind computerless desks, brandished laminated documents, drank bottled orange juice on yachts moored in the Hampshire drizzle and talked about *the marketing strategy* and *the business plan* and *the majority shareholders*, with as much logic and understanding as Patrick Stewart doing lines about tetrion particles and anti-matter coils.

The patriarch of the series, Tom Howard (played with monotone, cow-eyed earnestness by Maurice Colbourne), sank his redundancy money into a failing boatyard – and succeeded, despite the negativity of his new business partner Jack Rolfe (Glyn Owen), who spent most of his time out of his skull on whisky or snarling 'That's not a proper boat, a proper boat's made of wood' in a voice like ball bearings rolling around a bucket of phlegm. Tom's increasingly estranged wife, Jan (Jan Harvey) ran a world-renowned fashion house from a chandlery-cum-supermarket by the marina, and was frequently seen colouring in design sketches (done, off-screen, by Nicole Fahri) and having *Acorn Antiques*-standard phone conversations about 'contacts in Paris'. Her backer, Ken Masters (Stephen Yardley), the show's real hero, wore white roll-neck sweaters, drank spritzers and filled up his working day by making attempts to per-suade Jan to push her electric typewriter to one side and come out for lunch. (Their adulterous kiss in a Cannes hotel room, passing a strawberry from one mouth to another, may be the most disgusting sight on television before Ant and Dec made Paul Burrell their gimp by forc-ing him to eat caterpillars.)

In an echelon above them all, the excitingly amoral financier, Charles Frere (an essay in Cointreau-ad smoothness by Tony Anholt from *Space: 1999*) rode around in a big car telling his secretary to reschedule meetings and check flights to Geneva. His function in the plot was to be revealed as people's Real Father – and to bring the first season to a close by having sex with Tom and Jan Howard's daughter, Lynne (Tracey Childs, star of British TV's first tampon ad) and then being discovered nude on his yacht with a lady who looked like one of Bruce Forsyth's wives, but turned out to be someone called Mrs Honey Frere. In six long series not one of these characters had a plausible conversation about money.

And that's the value of *Howards' Way*. The meaninglessness of its boardroom arguments exposed the hollowness and banality of Thatcherism even as it celebrated its processes – and yet thirteen million tuned in each Sunday night. 'We joined the board of Railton Marine,' declared Jack Rolfe's sensible daughter, Avril (Susan Gilmore), in a climactic scene in a boat shed, 'who whilst manufacturing the Barracuda under franchise are also ensuring that new development finance is available . . .' Cockroaches, take note. This was us. The human race.

HBO Boxed Set Love – Sam Delaney

Tony Soprano is strangling Febby Petrulio using a piece of wire. Febby is thrashing about and croaking. His eyes bulge, his veins throb, his face turns puce. Tony is relentless, using all of his might to squeeze the last breath out of his one-time friend and colleague with a look of determined, murderous zest on his big, sweating face. As Febby's life finally ends, I take my wife's hand and squeeze it gently in a way that says: 'I love you. I love our life together. And perhaps most of all I love *The Sopranos*.' She squeezes back to show she concurs. It's a romantic moment. I think we both appreciate the crucial role that these New Jersey mobsters are playing in our marriage.

It is about nine o clock on a wet, wintry, Wednesday evening. We are relaxing on the bed, dressed in loose-fitting, elasticated comfort wear and eating tangerines. Our eight-month-old daughter is lying peacefully between us, murmuring in her sleep. She seems to love *The Sopranos* too but can rarely stay awake for more than one episode.

This is the face of the modern British family in 2009. At least it's the face of our family. When you're past thirty, you've got children that pretty much confine you to the home seven nights per week and your social life is dying a death more painful and drawn-out than even Febby Petrulio's, the humble DVD box-set is the only place you have to turn, other than perhaps booze and Valium.

Just as families of yore would gather round the wireless together *for Listen with Mother* or the latest rousing announcement from Mr Churchill, modern families gather round the DVD player and collectively immerse themselves in hour upon hour of high-end American TV drama. Or comedy. It doesn't really matter what genre it is as long as it begins with a fuzzy crackling image of the letters H, B and O. From *The Sopranos* to *The Wire* to *Sex and the City*, American subscription channel Home Box Office has been responsible for a slew of shows that, since the late nineties, have elevated television to a level of creativity currently unrivalled in popular culture. Previously thought of as the cheap, trashy, borderline moronic cousin of the Hollywood movie industry, television has now become the main source of classy, credible and innovative entertainment. And it's pretty much all thanks to HBO.

Because they are funded by viewer subscriptions, HBO don't have to rely on massive audiences or advertising revenue. This means they can afford to take gambles on seemingly preposterous TV ideas like *Curb Your Enthusiasm* (obnoxious Jewish writer spends long days doing nothing much) *or Flight of the Conchords* (two unemployed Kiwi musicians singing songs in New York) that would never make it through the sort of rigorous market-research procedures used by most entertainment companies. The pilot episode of *The Sopranos* flopped in focus group research. HBO commissioned the show and dropped the focus groups. *The Sopranos* became the most successful TV series of all time. The world became a better place.

Families are brought closer together by watching HBO box sets. Why would Dad stay out drinking with the lads when he could be at home watching season five of *The*

Wire with his wife? How could a wife possibly lose interest in a husband after watching every single episode of *Six Feet Under* with him? She couldn't: that kind of experience runs too deep. It entwines the souls. No wonder our own parents got divorced. The best they had in the seventies was *The Rockford Files*. And each time an episode of that ended they had to wait an entire week to find out what happened next. The frustration must have pushed them over the edge.

Of course, there are other shows that other people like to watch on DVD. Shows like *Heroes* or *Lost* or *24*. But they're not the same. They don't have the depth, the originality, the complexity or half the amount of rude words. They are just TV shows. HBO shows are something more: as their slogan rightly states: 'It's Not TV, It's HBO.'

Of course, I'm not really qualified to make these assumptions about those other shows. I've never seen any of them. Why? Because I am a TV snob, that's why. 'Did you see the new episode of *24* last night?' stupid, unsophisticated work colleagues ask me. 'No,' I smile in a twattish, patronising sort of way. 'I don't watch *24*. I watch *The Wire*. It's a treatise on the demise of the American dream which has been hailed by *The New Yorker* as the greatest show of all time, don't you know.' They look me up and down like I'm a dickhead and just shuffle off. I don't care.

I go home, change into my tracksuit and open a fresh box of *Deadwood* or *Oz* or *Entourage*. I cuddle my wife, press play on the remote and smile a smug little smile. We were raised to think that watching telly was lazy and rubbish. That it was a thicko's alternative to learning chess or practising the trumpet or reading a sodding book. But watching HBO shows has changed all that. Watching HBO shows makes you feel clever and cool and sexy.

More than that, they give you and your loved ones something to talk about other than the weather, the gas bill or whose turn it is to change the cat litter. They make a house a home. They are saving a whole generation of children from growing up in one-parent families. They say you can't buy love, romance or happiness. I say you can spend £120 on a complete box-set of *The Sopranos* and give it a damn good try.

Coming to Terms with Ourselves – Nicola Barr

You never think of the place where you grow up as strange, when you are there, growing up. But Northern Ireland in the late seventies and early eighties was, by any standards, not quite normal. I don't really mean the Troubles, which were there, constantly, but weren't weird to us because they always had been there. We assumed policemen carried machine guns all the time, we assumed it was normal to go through turnstiles to get into city centres. But we had these weird accents – all harsh consonants and flat vowels. I mean, not weird to us: but why did no one on TV sound like us? Normality had an English accent, and when, every so often, a Belfast accent would appear on *Why Don't You?* or an Antrim accent would pop up with a phone request on *Swap Shop*, we watched and listened with a mix of horror, shame and contempt, knowing they (and therefore we) sounded out of their depth, countrified, dumb, in comparison with our sleek English cousins.

These days, of course, it's supposed to be easier to get a telly presenting gig if you have rigorously maintained your regional accent and, what with James Nesbitt seeming to be the only actor used on ad voiceovers, the Northern Irish one is gradually losing its association with terms like 'remanded in custody'; 'controlled explosion'; 'political process'.

But in 1982, it was so very different. Northern Ireland was, as ever, in the news. The Republican hunger strikes in the Maze prison had been dominating the agenda for months. The Ulster Protestant working class saw themselves nowhere. Nor, I'm sure, was a lot of thought given to this absence.

Then BBC One screened the 'Billy Plays'.

The *Play for Today* series had been making waves for half a decade. Its one-hour-long plays, shown at prime-time, on the nation's most watched channel, were giving writers like Dennis Potter, Mike Leigh, David Hare and Alan Bleasdale the economic and creative freedom to produce gritty, leftist, stirring dramas. And into this slot appeared *Too Late to Talk to Billy*. The first in a trilogy of plays that was to become known, in lore, as the Billy Plays, it was written by Graham J. Reid (the other two were *A Matter of Choice for Billy* and *A Coming to Terms for Billy*). And it was set in a street in Belfast and it wasn't about the Troubles. It gave the Belfast-born Kenneth Branagh his first TV role, playing Billy Martin, the son who rubs up constantly against his hard-drinking father (James Ellis). The Martins were Protestants – loyalists, undoubtedly, but by no means consumed by politics. And Reid seemed consciously to place his play out of time. Outside events are not mentioned: this is the story of a family. A dysfunctional one, for sure – the mother has recently died of cancer and the father, a repressive, violent drunk, is off to England to look for work, leaving a raft of grievances and turmoil in his wake as his two grown-up children are left to look after their younger sisters. But the problems were socio-economic, and were problems being faced by working-class families throughout the UK.

I have little recollection of Billy, in actual time. I remember the tiny remote TV in the corner of our kitchen unusually staying on as we ate our tea (can it really have been shown at teatime? We ate our tea early in my house when I was young) and I remember the look of it: the living-room that seems preposterously small, now, for all the adults it contained. I remember an impossibly young Kenneth Branagh being shouted at and whacked by his drunken father, Norman. I remember a close-knit family yelling at each other, in glorious, harsh, strident Belfast accents. But most of all I remember then, and have remembered for years, my parents telling me to shush so they could watch in peace. It was TV people were talking about the next day and for days and weeks afterwards, water-cooler TV before anyone in Northern Ireland had ever set eyes on a water-cooler.

Was it seminal? Did it break boundaries, subvert all preconceived notions of a city known only on the mainland for its messy politics? Impossible to be subjective but it seems likely that the passionate affection my parents held for it was the excitement of members of a marginal misrepresented community seeing itself boldly and unapologetically represented on primetime TV. The same instinct that, despite everything that has changed, had them last winter zealously voting for Christine Bleakley on *Strictly Come Dancing* and Eoghan Quigg on *X Factor*. If nothing else, it made us feel a bit more normal.

Throughout the next two decades, there have been all too many real-life events in Northern Ireland that brilliant directors and writers have been able to plunder to produce groundbreaking drama-docs. Ulster's was a conflict particularly suited to TV, Hollywood movies never quite getting to the dark, grim heart of a conflict where killers rang the doorbell in provincial housing estates, walked in and shot men in their living rooms. With *Bloody Sunday* (2002) and *Omagh* (2004), Paul Greengrass produced two of the most heartbreaking, numbing dramas ever seen on TV. But really, not since Billy has there been a drama on primetime TV shown throughout the UK set in Ulster, about the lives of ordinary folk. Was it seminal? Oh yes.

The Naked Civil Servant Revisited
– Rupert Smith

The Naked Civil Servant, ITV's feature-length drama about the life of Quentin Crisp, was first broadcast on British television in December 1975 – at the time of writing, thirty-three years ago. Back then, it seemed like a turning point. For those of us growing up in the wake of the 1967 Sexual Offences Act, which partially decriminalised sex between men, it marked TV's first attempt to explore queer lives in a way that was neither disapproving nor depressing. It gave us our first gay screen hero, unforgettably interpreted by John Hurt. *The Naked Civil Servant* was radical, uncompromising drama, questioning sexuality and gender, celebrating difference and, in its elegant way, making no concessions to homophobes. Television had grown up. *Après Quentin*, we thought, *le déluge*.

But it was a false dawn. For the next three and a half decades, television drama has struggled with the subject of homosexuality. If there's one good drama with gay characters every couple of years, we count ourselves lucky. Commissioning editors at the major terrestrial channels shy away from proposals that contain more than a few peripheral queer characters. When we do see gay content in TV drama, it's usually part of deliberate diversity policy (as in soaps), or it's problematised in a way that wouldn't have seemed out of place in the fifties (see *Clapham Common*). Think this is an overstatement? Then name five British TV dramas in the last thirty years that have placed gay characters right at the centre, presented them as heroes and told stories about the gay experience. Not the 'gay best friend' experience, or the 'gay problem' experience, but what it actually feels like to live this life in these times. One: *Queer as Folk*. End of story.

Gay people tend to feature in TV drama as part of an ensemble. In *This Life* (1996–7), for instance, there was Warren and, when he left, bisexual Ferdy. In *Shameless* (2004–) there is the Lolita-ish son, Ian. In *Skins*, there's the over-achieving Maxxie. Soaps, cop shows and medical dramas are littered with gay characters, all getting on with the business of being part of the fabric of society. They're in the chorus line, seldom in the spotlight. The unique, revealing, inspiring stories of the gay world, of which Quentin Crisp's was just one, are not being told.

The Naked Civil Servant had a hard road from page to screen. Philip Mackie wrote the screenplay after several boozy lunches with Crisp; the script was turned down all over town until Jeremy Isaacs pushed it through at Thames Television. John Hurt was warned that it would destroy his career. It was shot on a modest budget over twenty-one days, and has since become one of the most celebrated of all television dramas. It rehabilitated Quentin Crisp, who was nearly sixty-seven at the time of transmission, and launched him on the international celebrity circuit. It did more to break down prejudice against homosexuals than almost anything else in the seventies, on or off the box – and, while it drew criticism for portraying gay men as effeminate, submissive creatures, it also became a rallying point for those who felt disenfranchised by the hyper-masculine, highly-sexualised, quasi-heterosexual model of homosexuality that was proliferating elsewhere.

Viewed today, *The Naked Civil Servant* is an astonishingly sharp, economical and comedic piece of television. Mackie's script, light as a feather, barely even tells a story – but it takes us right to the heart of Crisp's personal struggles in a series of impressionistic scenes, almost sketches, from the bedroom to the courtroom via endless shots in the mirror. It never engages with homosexuality as a subject for discussion – it presents it as a given, a fact to be accepted, celebrated even, and then focuses all its energy on presenting Quentin as a hero of individualism, pitted against the evil forces of the Crowd. It's not about *gay* v. *straight*. It's not about class war, or gender war, or any of the other faultlines of twentieth-century society. It's simply about *'us'* v. *'them'* – and nobody could watch Hurt as Crisp, heroically mincing through the West End and trying on lipstick, without feeling that he was 'one of us', and that you, perhaps, were 'one of them'.

That's the triumph of *The Naked Civil Servant* – it redrew the battle lines, and made millions of viewers who had never met a real live homosexual think that, after all, we were okay. That's something that can only be achieved by putting the queer experience centre stage, under the spotlight. It's all very well to show us as part of the wider picture – and certainly, soaps like *EastEnders* and *Coronation Street* have done a great deal of good by integrating homosexuals into their casts – but if we are ever to go beyond tolerance towards acceptance, inclusion and celebration, we need to tell those untold stories, to give our children gay heroes.

Now, thirty-three years after *The Naked Civil Servant*, and nearly a decade after *Queer as Folk*, we're still waiting. As I write at the end of 2008, I'm eagerly looking forward to a new drama that's promised from ITV for 2009, a drama that focuses entirely on the experience of one extraordinary, heroic, unique gay man. It's called *An Englishman in New York* – and it's the sequel to *The Naked Civil Servant*. And that will probably have to do for the next ten years.

Rubbish Bosses of TV – Christien Haywood

Nobody likes their boss. Whether they're giving you more work, carpeting you for *'erotic use of the teleconferencing suite'*, or refusing to give you an alibi for the police, bosses are rubbish. But spare a thought for the poor souls of TV; they have to deal with the very worst of bossdom. Lazy Bosses. Mental Bosses. *Shouty* Bosses. Bosses so awful it makes you like your own boss a little bit more, and regret spreading that rumour about them being on the Sex Offenders register. Some TV bosses are hapless, some TV bosses are hopeless, some TV bosses are downright terrifying, but they've all got one thing in common: they're all rubbish.

Take Paul Robinson from *Neighbours*. Paul Robinson was a terrible boss for a number of reasons. Firstly, he was convinced that nobody understood how important things were to Lassiters Leisure Complex. 'Have you *ANY* idea how important this is to Lassiters?!' he'd hiss to employees three or four thousand times a day, spittle flecking his chops. That kind of behaviour would get on your wick almost immediately. Secondly, he was clearly not too bright. He married one woman Christina Alessi then later had an affair with her *identical twin sister* Caroline. Pointless. Finally, and most importantly, there was his overwhelming obsession with the (probably imaginary) Mr Udegawa who was apparently the only investor in the whole world. In all the years he has been in the series, Paul had over 20,000 off-screen 'meetings' with Mr Udegawa, which clearly drove him insane and turned him into the Colonel Kurtz of the hospitality industry. Paul has had dozens of assistants since becoming the hotel manager. To date not one of them has grasped how important a thing is – or things are – to Lassiters.

In a similar vein we have Dev from *Coronation Street*. How can you explain his bizarre behaviour, the wild eye-rolling, the sudden bouts of 'hilarity', the odd pronunciation, the singing? He acts like a man constantly inhaling nitrous oxide (probably bought from The Kabin. Norris strikes me as a man who could lay his hands on that sort of thing, if you ask me). Dev is clearly not of this world, as he probably spends most of his time thinking of the oddest way to say 'HelLO there, RiTA' when she walks into his shop. Being around Dev would make you fear for your sanity. If you worked for him, you'd go batty quicker than spit.

So let's leave the present, and voyage into the future: the twenty-fifth century to be precise, where we join the satin-jumpsuited Buck Rogers talking to his boss – the President of Earth, Dr Elias Huer. Now *he* sounds like a man of action, doesn't he? A real 'take-charge' kind of boss? Someone who you'd look up to, and seek advice from? Uh, *kinda* . . . Overwhelming simpering and colossal indecisiveness in the face of global emergencies mean that Dr Huer is one of the worst bosses ever, and probably a bedwetter too. A middle-aged gent uncompromisingly squeezed into a tight flightsuit, Dr Huer never found a difficult decision he couldn't look scared of while simultaneously looking a bit fey. He generally only ever had one line – a nervous 'Oooh – what do you think, Buck?', leaving poor old bloody Buck to sort everything out while Dr Huer had a nice camomile tea. God only knows how Huer managed to get elected as Ruler of the

World in the first place, although the fact the Earth was a zombie-infested radioactive wasteland probably helped.

The universe is a big place – surely there's got to be a more decisive boss out there *some*where? James T. Kirk of the Starship *Enterprise* is fun to be around. Each day brings a new challenge, whether it's wrestling with your Evil Dimension twin, discovering you have no face or suddenly ageing a hundred years in a second. Kirk even seems like a charismatic boss – always leads from the front and brings Krispy Kremes in on a Friday if his waistline is anything to go by. But there's a downside. Do the maths: the USS *Enterprise* had, on its five year mission, a crew of just under five hundred; during those five years, Captain Kirk was responsible for the deaths of pretty much every crewmember, especially if you wore a red shirt. God *alone* knows what their recruitment drives were like. So, Captain Kirk: great people skills, but as for collecting your pension? Forget it.

Let's consider law enforcement. Chief O'Hara from *Batman*. He combines the bewilderment of Dr Huer with the incompetence of Dev. If you need a boss to get confused and look like a panic-stricken bulldog then Chief O'Hara is the man for you. He's no use as a policeman – he's barely any use as a human being – and it's clearly just the simmering sexual tension between him and Commissioner Gordon that's keeping him in a job.

How about Boss Hogg from *The Dukes of Hazzard*? Maybe he's a good boss? He's certainly very forgiving towards Sheriff Roscoe P. Coltrane, who drove his police car into a ditch (in slow motion) dozens of times during the course of the series. Regrettably Boss Hogg was a colossal pervert. I know, you'd never guess it from his name. You know that immaculate white suit he used to wear all the time? He made Roscoe and Cletus *clean it with their tongues* every day. How about Charlie from *Charlie's Angels*? Let's see, he only hires hot women, he calls them 'little girls' in the opening titles and we never see him, we only ever hear him on speakerphone. In fact, we have no idea what he's doing in there when he's speaking with the Angels. What is he *doing* in there?

We need a boss with a solid moral centre. Someone religious, like Tripitaka from *Monkey*, perhaps? Ostensibly a peace-loving Buddhist, this gentle soul commands the respect of his student Monkey through kindness, wisdom and a skull-crushing metal headband which contracts if Monkey is disobedient. I bet there wasn't a mention of that at the job interview. Tripitaka, a male character, is played by a quite sexy woman, which has got to be a little confusing at work.

It's pretty clear that there are no decent bosses on TV. They're all bastards. But how could I forget Freddie from *Scooby-Doo*? Yes, I know he's only a cartoon character, but he *is* a boss (more or less) and he's definitely a lovely guy. As no one appears to have jobs in this cartoon, the only explanation is that monster hunting actually *is* their job. Freddie is a good-looking, clean-cut, kindly boss always concerned for his 'employees'. He always comes to the aid of Shaggy and Scooby, and pays them a regular wage of Scooby Snacks. He rewards independent problem solving and always gives credit where it's due too. What a top boss.

Except, their job is largely unpaid and extremely dangerous; the 'office' is a stinking van which the human employees have to share with a talking dog who has a speech impediment; and he often uses them all as bait to catch some terrifying Radioactive Gorilla Monster, then swoops in to take all the credit. Worst and most transparent of all, a typical plan from Freddie might be that the team should split up to look for, say, the Fiery Fish Ghost, and he and Daphne will 'investigate' in the attic. You can practically hear him unzipping himself as he says it.

Oh, Freddie. Dirty boy. And another bad boss.

5

Electrickery:
TV Invades Real Life

In which TV makes you sick, develop phobias and cry, listings magazines spark World War III, one man loses it when faced with the neighbours from hell and another turns up in fancy dress as a TV character he's never even seen before.

It's amazing how, if you're not careful, TV inveigles its way into the rest of your day. One moment you're able to hold a decent adult conversation, the next all you can do is reel off catchphrases from *The Fast Show* in the hole where once conversation used to be. This chapter is full of more personal stories, so please allow me to demonstrate how telly invaded one very important aspect of my life.

Television hasn't so much had an effect on my life so much as alternately ruined and saved it. Take our junior school play, a production of *The Little Mermaid* back in the days before Disney defeated the whole point of the story by giving it a happy ending. I was nine. It was a mixed school, but even so I was given the part of the Sea Witch which I was to play with two other boys under a giant sheet. Dr Freud, your services are no longer required. The director, our bully of a deputy head called Mr Bell, was determined we should get into character and spent a great deal of time coaching us to the heights of junior acting ability seldom seen beyond the confines of the Sylvia Young Theatre School. I wasn't sure how to play a witch, especially one who spoke only every third line from under a sheet, so I turned to telly for my inspiration. In 1979 there was only one obvious role model. Servalan from *Blake's Seven* was pure evil in mules. She had a very particular way of speaking which I, the budding young de Niro, attempted to emulate. Sentences would begin with a single word shot out like a bullet, and followed by a modulated purr sprinkled with a liberal helping of pausing and pouting. Needless to say I was a natural and it went down very well in rehearsals, even Mr Bell was impressed. However, come the first night he clearly thought I needed some extra help. Before we three witches went on he spent some time telling us exactly how we should play the scene, and in a sudden about-face I was told that my Servalan act wasn't working. With no time to perfect a convincing Hazel the McWitch (I don't do accents) I was shoved under my sheet and the scene started. Without the aid of Servalan I was all at sea, and when we came off stage the three of us nine-year-olds stood before Mr Bell as he told us we'd ruined his play. Oh Servalan, we were so good together, only to be torn apart by a cruel twist of fate, and a teacher who looked like Tosh from *The Bill*.

I didn't fare much better at the comprehensive, especially at sport, for which the blame falls squarely on the padded shoulders of Stephanie Powers. *Hart to Hart* was a big show on Sunday nights. In Aaron Spelling's world glamorous millionaires have nothing better to do than solve crimes, rather than, as the news has taught us, to commit them. There may have been a better role model on Sunday night telly for a twelve-year-old boy at a rough comprehensive in Croydon than Jennifer

'she's gawjaws' Hart, but I wasn't aware of one.
Compo? Harry Secombe? Arthur Negus? I think not.
And I just wasn't Robert Wagner material. So Stephanie
Powers it was, and I channelled that neckerchiefed mil-
lionairess where it mattered most: in indoor cricket.
Mrs H did a lot of running – mainly away from grizzled
gunmen over moored yachts or Dobermanns in the
grounds of mansions – and indoor cricket required a lot
of running too. She was my running icon, the very
incarnation of all things in a hurry. So I took my place
to bat, a shy beanpole in plimsolls facing a gym full of
boys more hyena than human, and the PE teacher yelled
out 'Big hitter!' to much laughter from the assembled
animals. 'Right,' I thought. 'I'll show 'em.' To everyone's amazement I hit the ball and started running, with
Stephanie Powers as my spirit guide. Only problem was,
she does that kind of flappy 'jazz hands' running your
aunt might do if she had to tell her husband he needed
to move their Allegro in a hurry at a wedding. And so,
at that moment, did I. Better still, I scored a run!
Perhaps because everyone in the gym was rolling on the
floor laughing, most particularly the teacher. Again:
'Big hitter!' Whack! Jazz hands jazz hands. And again.
And again. Pretty soon I'd amassed the best score I'd
ever reached in any sport, and Jennifer Hart was my
coach. My team won, I was their star player, and I think
the other boys learned just a smidgeon of respect for me
at that moment that lasted all through school. No, of
course they didn't.

I think we can all see where these stories are leading. It
was only a matter of time before I decided to come out to
my parents as the dirty gaylord that Servalan and Jennifer

Hart had made me. It's one of the more humiliating scenarios life had to offer me as an appallingly naïve and inhibited teenager, to go to my parents and introduce the topic of my deviant sex life to them. 'So, Mum and Dad, that is the extent of my knowledge of anilingus – any questions?' But before I could even get round of thinking of how to phrase it, I had to pick the right moment. The key was to make it a non-event. Their wedding anniversary was out, then. It had to be the most uneventful day of the year, at the dullest possible moment. Which is how I came to tell my parents during an ad break in *Taggart*. Not during *Taggart*, mind, that could have ruined everything, but during the ads. My thinking was quite clear: Mum and Dad loved a good *Taggart*, so they'd be in the same place at the same time; they wouldn't want to spoil the episode by talking too much, so the ad break created a perfect and finite window; and if it was a good episode they could get straight back into the story again and it would be barely as if their youngest son had just blurted out his love for anal sex. And, I am pleased to tell you, the plan worked perfectly. It was almost as if they had suspected it. I have no idea how. My Dad mumbled something about it being a phase, but my Mum told him to shut up, and then those familiar gritty electric guitar chords played and all eyes returned to the screen. I love it when a plan comes together.

The following year I was electrocuted by full mains voltage from our TV, but that's another story.

Sick TV – Sam Delaney

Mum was at work. My older brother, who had been granted a day off secondary school in order to keep an eye on me, had quickly resigned his duties and headed round his mate's house for a spot of solvent abuse. My packed lunch box sat on the table next to me with a steaming cup of Lemsip beside it. I turned the gas fire to maximum, shuffled over to the Granada-rented, teak-finished TV set in the corner of the room and pressed the power button. By the time I was back on the sofa, stretched out in my jim-jams and dressing gown, the black dusty screen had slowly awakened from its slumber and I was ready to enjoy my sick-day TV marathon.

The Waltons, The Sullivans, Sons and Daughters, Knots Landing and, of course, *Crown Court*. These were the shows that would accompany the malingering school children of mid-eighties Britain. While superficially varied in their themes and settings, they were united under the same woozy and depressing atmosphere that prevailed across all four channels throughout daytime hours. Had I watched them under different circumstances, without my senses dulled by viral infection, Lemsip and that gas fire, might I have assessed them differently? No. The daytime TV of that era was, by any objective analysis, shit.

The Waltons? A load of destitute hicks titting about up a mountain. Pa forever fixing the car in those daft dungarees, Grandma Walton with her sanctimonious, home-spun moralising and John Boy going on about getting one of his rubbish stories published in the local rag. God, I hated that moley-faced spod. He might have fancied himself as a brainbox but, when push came to shove, all he did with his rotten life was enlist in the military and get his plane shot down in the war. I bet he didn't feel so clever then, did he?

Then there was *The Sullivans*: more of the same dreary accounts of ordinary folk doing ordinary stuff in the olden days, only this time in Australia. Uncle Harry's got a new job; Kitty's got a boyfriend; Grace has died in an air raid during her trip to London; Dad's lost his hat. Who cared? Not me. So why did I watch? Because I was off school, I was lazy, there was no remote control and all that was on the other side was the stupid test card anyway. *The Sullivans* and *The Waltons* might have been boring but that demented clown and his strange, grinning girlfriend were just plain scary. So scary in fact, that I would occasionally become a little bit paranoid about being in the house all on my own. If I went upstairs for a wee, might that gruesome double-act be waiting to smash me over the head with their noughts and crosses blackboard and feed me chalk? Probably best I remained in front of the telly and didn't move until Mum got home, just in case.

All those shows with their bad acting and wobbly sets might have been crappy but they were at least familiar and comforting. Like *The Sullivans*, *Sons and Daughters* was a hit Australian soap that was used to pad out the daytime schedule in Britain. It took the idea of the prosaic, repetitive soap opera to its illogical extremes, featuring loads of unattractive Aussie actors with bad haircuts and clothes in every shade of brown sitting about in tastelessly furnished living rooms having conversations about what to have for tea. Plus, it had the most sadden-

ing, mournful titles sequence of any television programme ever made. A montage of sepia-toned headshots
of the cast played out to a wailing theme tune which
opened with the words 'Sons and Daughters, love and
laughter, tears and sadness and happineeeessss . . .' Just
thinking about it makes me want to cry. They could have
opened the show with an image of a kitten slowly suffo-
cating in a clear plastic bag to the strains of 'The End' by
The Doors and it wouldn't have been any more sad.

Mind you, if it was upbeat, exhilarating opening titles
you wanted then the daytime schedule could provide
them elsewhere thanks to the American soaps *Knots
Landing* and *Falcon Crest*. One was about the
Californian wine industry; the other was a *Dallas* spin-
off starring a young Alec Baldwin. Both opened with
sweeping helicopter shots of vast, glamorous-looking
landscapes to the accompaniment of frenzied, sax-driven,
funk-symphonies. But which was which? Nobody knew.
All that mattered was that a woman with an impressive
manicure would slap a square-jawed gentleman in a
sports jacket round his smug face towards the end of
every episode and say something like 'That baby is mine
and I intend to keep it.'

These shows might have been terrible but they were
also somehow hypnotic, offering a grim portal into the
mysteries of adult life. Was this really the sort of crap
they got up to during the day when we were at school? If
it was, then I didn't want to ever grow up. Especially
after watching an episode of *Crown Court*, the bleak,
hyper-realistic drama in which genuine members of the
public would act as jurors in a dramatised criminal trial.
It was a concept far too complex for my juvenile mind to

grasp: I just thought it was live coverage from real-life courtrooms. Courtrooms that dealt with murder, rape and kidnap trials. Courtrooms in which the guilty would get off scot-free and the innocent would be sentenced to life and dragged down to the cells in floods of tears. All this at midday on a Wednesday afternoon! As the spirit-crushing theme tune played over the closing titles I would fight back the tears and curse the injustices of the grown-up world. Then I'd look at the clock, realise that playtime was about to start back at school and vow never, ever to pull a sickie again.

Unexpectedly Moving Adverts – Colin Harvey

I grew up a repressed southern bloke, and advertisements taught me everything I needed to know about the emotional side of life. Now, let's face it, we aren't meant to be moved by ads – and if we are, we're probably not meant to admit it. But this belies the genuine affection the public – and by the term 'public' I mean 'me' – feel for some telly adverts. I'm not talking here about the ironic affection with which, say, Barry Scott is regarded or the ambassador's balls are held. No, what I'm talking about is a genuine love felt for certain campaigns.

Nimble Bread's 'Up, Up and Away' advert from 1974 is probably my first televisual memory, and as such one of my first memories full-stop. A beautiful woman dressed as an air hostess is strapped into the harness of a hot-air balloon which gaily lifts off the ground and floats over mountainous terrain to the sound of 'Can't Let Maggie Go'. At the end of the advert, still floating, she proceeds to eat a sandwich. As a kid it gave me insight into the mysterious, exciting world of grown-ups, where people evidently travelled via their own personal balloons, but still had the foresight to bring a packed lunch.

The famous R Whites Lemonade campaign – perhaps *the* signature ad of the 1970s – offered me similar insights into the peculiar parallel universe inhabited by adults. A bespectacled man, addicted to lemonade, makes a night-time trip to the fridge for his latest fix, all the time singing about the object of his fascination. In perhaps the most momentous reveal since the invention of cinema, closing the refrigerator presents him with his puzzled-looking wife. Quite why she is so mystified is anyone's guess, as forensic inspection of the ad reveals that the couple apparently keep *five* large bottles of lemonade in their fridge as a matter of course. (Maybe she hadn't noticed: they often say relatives of junkies live in a state of denial.) The husband breaks out of song to offer, by way of explanation, 'R Whites Lemonade', and realisation dawns on the wife's face. Just like Nimble, the ad seemed to provide some kind of clue as to the mysterious activities of grown-ups: my dad wore pyjamas, my mum wore a nightdress, ergo imbibing vast quantities of lemonade must be what they got up to at night.

Elsewhere in the seventies, Tufty the squirrel was exploring an existential landscape reminiscent of Sartre's *Huis Clos*. Sure, there were buildings and other characters – what's that for Chrissake, a *stoat*? – but otherwise Tufty inherited a sterile environment far removed from the intricate, warm *mise en scène* of legit animated characters like *Mr Benn* or *The Wombles*. The irony was that this was a road safety campaign shot in a world where there were hardly any vehicles. To a child, this only made the tragedy of those stop-frame rodents all the more affecting: as Sartre almost nearly said, to be run down by a car on an otherwise empty road is truly moving.

The 1980s are not a decade known for warmth and fuzziness, but in an era where individuals had supposedly supplanted society, families continued to dominate telly ads. At face value the long-running Oxo Family campaign seemed to challenge the preconceived wisdom that advertising sells aspiration. Here they were, a bald father sporting a compensatory moustache, a chubby daughter, lanky son and a son so nondescript he wasn't even lanky, presided over by a matriarchal Lynda

Bellingham, forever cuffed in a pair of oven mitts. In actual fact, this family was so far removed from my own experience that I may as well have been watching *The Jetsons*. Sure, these people squabbled, but such conflicts were invariably resolved by the emergence of a steaming plate of shepherd's pie. And not just by someone throwing it. If only all family disagreements could really be solved by thin beef stock, that would make Relate's job considerably easier.

Elsewhere, *Yellow Pages* reinvented English social realism for the era of palpitating excess. A young Northern lad sits on his parents' porch gazing longingly at a picture of a racing bike while his Northern dad towers over him and criticises his son's lamentable taste. Inside, Northern dad confers with Northern mum who confirms she has located a mysterious undisclosed object. Cue fruity voiceover telling us *Yellow Pages* isn't just there for the nasty (and presumably, southern) things in life. Northern dad watches Northern lad pedalling off on inappropriate bicycle from crafty vantage point, and Northern dad can't resist having the last word. God, I wish I was Northern.

Fast-forward to the 1990s: a sobbing brunette arrives on a cliff side in her Volkswagen Beetle, obviously the victim of some callous relationship-smashing bastard. Perhaps the Beetle is the only reliable thing in her life – but no, wait! Poking out of her bag she spies a jar of Nescafé. To the tune of 'I Can See Clearly Now the Rain Has Gone' she boils herself a cup of coffee, courtesy of a plug-in element. We see her sipping from the mug and admiring the beautiful sky and know that things will be okay from now on, now that she has caffeine racing through her bloodstream. Just as long as she doesn't flatten the car battery and end up murdered.

And now, here I am, a parent myself, tears brimming through Persil's 'Dirt is Good' campaign. An archetypal toy robot wanders out into the rain and gradually begins to emulate the mannerisms of a child, before *transforming* into a child. The clincher moment, the one that really makes me blub, is when the robot-kid swings his arms back and forth in a puddle. Precisely one million times more profound than the entirety of *AI: Artificial Intelligence*.

So what have adverts taught me about life, love, emotion? Well, now I'm a respectable married man with two children and a fixed-rate mortgage, I realise the secret of being an emotionally competent human being was there all along: when attempting a solo balloon flight always have the foresight to prepare a packed lunch.

I Should've Gone as Velma: Or, How I Learned to Stop Worrying about *Byker Grove* and Love *Bagpuss* – Andrew Benbow

I don't get out much. Television is my life: all of my thinking has been programmed from an Antipodean youth misspent bathing in the cathode rays of what I believed to be the best TV the UK and the US had to offer. My impressionable young mind received its education devouring a warped diet of escapist transatlantic transmissions. I graduated from the coolest of kids' programmes through to the most reassuring of sitcoms. I was mentally well equipped for anything life could throw at me. I was prepared to become an Afro-American orphan adopted into a rich whiter-than-white Sacramento-based travelling band of a family; for the hassle of keeping a sea monster hidden in my beach hut; or to celebrate the saving of my favourite condemned playground tree by eating a vast amount of cartoon bangers and mash.

As I grew, I struggled to find a place in the real world where I could utilise the knowledge those wonder years had furnished me with. It doesn't happen often in life that an opportunity arises to go back to that place where people remember you for the genius you were once threatening to become, but for me that opportunity arrived in the form of an invite from my workmate, Tony, to a TV fancy dress party in the year 2000. It was time to reclaim my youth.

At first I thought I could wear my *Regal Beagle* T-shirt and go as *Three's Company*'s Jack Tripper but my hair was thinning and I couldn't afford the kind of luscious rug required to pull off the seventies US leading man

look. Maybe I could go as Jack's landlord, Mr Furley –
camp it up big time with a loud paisley shirt and an
orchid lei . . . *Shit! Fuck!* I suddenly realised that no one
at an English party would know who the hell I was trying to be. One of the harshest lessons I have learned over
the years is that 'best of British and American TV' that I
had digested in my youth often turned out to be nothing
more than cheap and unfashionable fare foisted upon an
unsuspecting third-world country.

'Why don't thee go as P.G. 'n' Dooncan from *Burkha
Grave*, like?' offered my Northern flatmate, Oz (I say
'Northern' but I was beginning to suspect that his accent
was a put-on, or that I was actually imagining it from
having watched too many BBC Brontë adaptations).

'Yeah, maybe . . .' I replied, not wanting to let him
know that I didn't have a clue what *Burkha Grave* was. I
pretended that I had other eggs hatching and moved
away, slowly to the safety of my room to think alone. It
came to me the next evening when Oz and his girlfriend
Nora and I were watching *The Simpsons* – I could go as
Gilligan, the goofy first mate from *Gilligan's Island*! All I
needed was a white sailor's hat, a red top, some white
shorts and a tattoo with 'The Minnow' emblazoned over
a watery blue love-heart . . . I mean, if something is referenced on *The Simpsons*, and everyone in the room
laughs, then everyone knows the show, right?

Nora helped me bake a cake and didn't even question
me when I said it had to read 'Happy Birthday, MaryAnn
XoX!' She even applied my tattoo as requested. She had
said that she could have 'borrowed me' one of her wigs
and she could've made me up to look 'just like Velma
from *Scooby-Doo*, pet'. She hadn't seen *Gilligan's Island*

but told me she were brought up in a broadcast region that was missing a channel. When I said that it was like a cooler version of *The Love Boat* meets *Fantasy Island* she went, 'Sure, yeah, okay like,' and I saw that as a green light for a successful evening to come.

The night arrived. I turned up soaking wet. I'd lost my hat, my tattoo had run and the cake was a disaster. The icing had blurred under the cling film to read what looked like 'What's the New Mary Jane?' I was met at the door by a very attractive androgynous-looking type with dark slicked-down hair, a blazer and white cricket trousers. She raised an eyebrow at my pathetic appearance and muttered a 'Thanks, I s'pose' at the corpse of a cake I proffered. 'Come in out of the rain, Mork!' It took a few seconds for me to realise that she was mistaking my red top and corduroys (not quite vintage Gilligan but as close as I could get). I quickly scanned myself to make sure that I hadn't mysteriously turned up as a wacky alien as my glum hostess disappeared into the ether – or kitchen, more likely. I saw Tony, dressed as Fred from *Scooby-Doo* talking to a Penelope Pitstop. It hit me that maybe I should've came as Velma after all. Tony beckoned me over with a smug 'Nanoo, Nanoo'. I asked him about the girl who had met me at the door and was handing out vol-au-vents.

'Oh, that's Number Six. It's her party. You should go over and talk to her – the whole moody thing is just the character. She's actually really lovely.' I decided to try my luck. Perhaps we'd just got off on the wrong foot.

'So you're Number Six? That's my lucky number.' She looked at me coldly for a moment, smiled and then shouted in my face 'I am not a number!' and stormed off, leaving me completely embarrassed, confused but also slightly aroused. She certainly held character well. I was about to follow when I noticed that her identical twin was entering the room from another door. I caught the eye of this new Number Six, who looked even more cruelly androgynous and alluring. She was holding what appeared to be a cardboard cut out of an old bicycle but I couldn't afford to let that put me off. If anything, it only added to the mystery.

Even though I knew that she was probably looking at my costume, thinking 'Nice look, Mork!' I felt that I should muster the courage of an already rejected fool and approach her, using many of the great TV lines I had stored in my head. I decided that the simple goofy 'Hi, I'm Mork!' would suffice. It kind of worked. We (reluctantly on her part) entered into a conversation about *Prisoner*. I told her about how I used to come home from school and my mum would be ironing whilst watching the show. I found the whole scenario quite sinister. On screen, Bea would always be telling someone that she was 'top dog' and that they should 'rack off' and leave Birdsworth alone, whilst jamming the oversized industrial iron down on some poor inmate.

'You mean *Prisoner: Cell Block H*!' interrupted a pitiful creature, dressed in a shabby fluffy pink and white cat costume. Number Six no. 2 sneered and disappeared in an instant, leaving me hemmed in with no escape, listening to the weird human fur ball wittering on, whilst disconcertingly holding a large cat head under her right arm, one gauzy eye staring up at me from a weird angle. I didn't know where to look or which face to reply to.

'Over here it was called *Prisoner: Cell Block H* so as

not to be confused with . . .' As her monologue went on I feigned interest and watched my chances dwindle of getting off with either Number Six, who had locked lips to make a twelve, disappear. For the second time in the evening I thought to myself, 'I should've come as Velma.'

I considered asking cat girl if she'd like a drink, thinking that I would be able to slip unnoticed out of the hallway door and be home in time to watch the midnight repeat of *Magnum P.I.* But, just as I was about to unleash my devious plan, she leaned in conspiratorially and purred, 'So, you thought you could escape your Island and come here as Gilligan?'

It turned out that she had spent two months visiting her cousins in Australia when she was ten, and had become addicted to *Gilligan's Island*, so much so that she wouldn't stop talking about it to her school friends when she got back to England. After a couple of weeks she had considerably fewer friends. Here was a girl who had suffered for a cause dear to my heart. I suddenly started to notice things about her that I had been too blind to see before, like the fact that her eyes were ever so slightly off line, in the most heartbreakingly cute way possible. I forgot all about the eeriness of the sewn-on cat's head protruding from her side.

We spent the next couple of hours talking TV. Well, she did most of the talking while I tried to think who it was she had come to the party as. The lack of a boater ruled out Top Cat, but maybe Choo-choo or another of the gang? Surely not the Cat in the Hat? Scratchy? She was too pink-striped for Tom, and too grey-striped for Roobarb (was Roobarb even a cat?). For a short time my mind chased its own tail, but after a while I just stared dreamily and dumbly at her eyes, smiling. It was only after she left that I realised that I hadn't asked. I looked down at the piece of paper she had written her number on, half expecting to find the truth revealed in brackets after her real name, Emily.

As it turned out I never did call.

When I got home Oz and Nora came out of their bedroom, like parents who had spent the whole night waiting up for me. When I related the events of the evening, they both laughed and told me that I had 'gotten off with Bagpuss!' I had kind of lied about the getting-off bit. To console me they said that only someone with pitifully low self-esteem would go to a party dressed as Bagpuss – she probably had serious weight or mental issues, or something even worse. I tried not to believe them, I tried to be strong and not succumb to peer pressure, but when I went down to Record and Tape and purchased a second hand VHS of *Bagpuss*, I realised that I would never be able to call sweet adorable Emily. As soon as I saw the weird movements, the saucer-shaped head and heard the creepy sounds, I knew that I could never be alone with her without the laughter of my flatmate and Bagpuss's menacing voice echoing in my head.

Irrational Childhood Fears from TV – Ben Rawson-Jones

Never underestimate the impact of television on impressionable minds. It can function as a great educational tool, but away from the sticky-backed plastic world of *Blue Peter* there are many corrupting forces at work. This was especially the case in the 1980s, when certain moments on the box had a very adverse effect on one particular viewer who was barely spoke-high to a BMX. Here are the life-shattering phobias that emerged . . .

Picnics

Neighbours was famed for its stunning cliffhangers, but one turned the great outdoors into an exclusion zone for me. The scene featured a red-backed spider invading a family picnic in the woods, somehow bypassing Harold Bishop's jelly belly to sink its fangs into Joe Mangel's helpless daughter. Every picnic site, no matter how sterile it appeared, would consequently be treated as a crime scene in the making. Admittedly, the menace in question was an indigenous beast not known to British shores – but try explaining to a trembling child that red-backed spiders don't have a UK visa. *Neighbours* hardly did wonders for the natural world. What was the heavily pregnant Kerry Mangel's reward for protesting against a duck hunt? Death by stray bullet. Presumably Bouncer's rabies-fuelled Ramsay Street rampage was cut out in the editing suite.

Elderly Relatives

The ravages of time are unavoidable, especially back in the pre-Botox age. So spare a thought for my poor grandmother, who bore an uncanny facial resemblance to *Doctor Who* villain, Dalek creator Davros. They shared the same bulging veins, withered eyelids, droopy jowls and mobility issues. She looked at her grandson with tender, unconditional love. He gazed back waiting for a glowing blue eye to sprout from her forehead. Every time she called him over to hand him a Werther's Original he thought she was summoning him for extermination. Let's not even discuss the poor aunt who had an unfortunate resemblance to Zelda from *Terrahawks* . . .

Haircuts

The eighties were dominated by follicular disasters, but mullet-related fears weren't why I had to be dragged kicking and screaming to the barbers. Those bloody *Tripods* were to blame, as the three-legged foes enslaved the earth by 'capping' – a mind-control process that involved freshly shaven humans having a metal mind-control cap meshed into their bald bonces. This meant plenty of scenes of hysterical youngsters having their locks forcefully hacked off as a precursor to losing their identity. After witnessing such imagery, tantrums would inevitably accompany a trip to the hairdresser. For once, the mandatory tissue handed to you after the shearing actually came in handy – to mop up the tears. The Tripods are coming . . .

Weddings

Nothing could redeem the institution of marriage after the

infamous Moldavian Wedding Massacre in *Dynasty*. The ceremony started beautifully, but as soon as the vows were exchanged, some random SWAT team burst through the church windows and gunned them all down. Not even their shoulder pads could offer much protection to the guests. I made a vow to tell any prospective fiancée that matrimony would only take place in a tiny registry office with metal bars over the windows and an alligator-filled moat surrounding the premises. Still, if only that Moldavian SWAT team received an invite to Kylie and Jason's wedding on *Neighbours* – they could have drowned out that ghastly soft rock soundtrack with gunfire.

Birth

Welcoming new life into the world should be a joyous experience, but a gruesome scene in American sci-fi series *V* ensured that I'd view the entire process of reproduction with extreme suspicion. In the show, one woman gets up the duff after a quick roll in the hay with a malevolent space lizard – albeit while he was disguised as a hunk in fake human skin. To everyone's horror, when it came to labour out popped a snarling baby reptile. Nice. What was inspirational material for David Icke was life-changing for me. When the fruit of my loins is born one day, you can be sure I'll be buying some live mice instead of rusks just in case.

Flying

Air travel can be a fairly stomach-churning experience, so the big smiley face on the titular cartoon plane in *Jimbo and the Jet Set* should have eased my fears. Alas, along came an episode where Jimbo flew off into the eerie Bermuda Triangle and encountered a graveyard full of crashed old planes. Great, just what you need to see as a nipper about to head off with the family on some cheap package holiday.

Singing

Public displays of vocal harmony have never recovered from the Rod, Jane and Freddy effect. As if the mime sequences and wispy mullets weren't bad enough, their songs were so patronising it was hard not to spit out the dummy in disgust while watching *Rainbow*. No wonder Zippy always had the hump (and a bit of Bungle if you tap into certain post-modern readings of the show).

Art

I wasn't really bothered about 'Allo 'Allo turning the Gestapo into figures of fun. After all, it was a good few years before my History A level taught me that Von Smallhausen didn't play a legitimate part in the Third Reich. But growing up in a sexually repressed household where my mother would regularly deface page three of the *Sun* with a black marker pen, Herr Flick's desperation to find *The Fallen Madonna with the Big Boobies* raised the taboo subject of large mammaries. A painful amount of blushing ensued, followed by a swift excuse to leave the room until the art attack subsided.

Swimming

Aquatic activities were strictly off the agenda after the events of a late eighties *Doctor Who* adventure in which companion Bonnie Langford took a dip in the pool of the sinister Paradise Towers. Before the serial shrieker knew it, she was being menaced by a bug-eyed robotic crab with metallic pincers that silently emerged from the depths. The killer crab was hardly Jaws, and seemingly fashioned from a vacuum cleaner and traffic cones, but proved effective enough to make me bin my trusted water-wings and steer clear of the shallowest of waters. It just goes to show that the power of imagination can turn even the most sedate bits of plastic into the greatest threat ever. Just ask Peter Andre.

Life

Much effort was made into giving *EastEnders* a gritty realism when it first hit the air in 1985, but art trying to imitate life quickly became art trying its hardest to put me off life. Was it fair to expose a fresh-faced kiddy to a world littered with endless sour-faced scowls, punch-ups, prostitution, drug dependency and worst of all – Ian Beale? I was helplessly engulfed by the morbid stench of Albert Square and feared for the future. Perhaps this explained why all the children's presenters were so nauseatingly cheerful – they needed to function as some kind of televisual Prozac to stop the nation's youth from pedalling their BMXs over the nearest cliff.

Having endured such telly trauma over my formative years, it's a miracle I'm in a position to write this piece. Things are different nowadays, with the box in the corner of my room offering a constant source of comfort away from the harsh extremities of life. I put it all down to the dramatic growth of Reality TV. Simply switch on any of those shows, observe the contestants and think 'Thank God that's not me.' As far as reconciliations go between man and machine, it's bliss.

Neighbourhood Watch – Jonathan Carter

I'm not sure how much more of this I can take. There I was again last night, about to turn over and go to sleep, when he starts up outside. That damned neighbour of ours, shouting his head off. It's the same story every time. He puts the cat out, the door closes behind him, and he shouts 'Wiiiiilmaaaa' at the top of his voice until he wakes the whole neighbourhood. I don't know how that poor wife of his puts up with it.

When he first started doing it, I put a note through his letterbox: 'Dear Mr Flintstone, Kindly cease your bawling at all hours. Please remember to put your door on the latch.' But did it help? No. So I went down and told him exactly what I thought. I pointed out that there was in fact no glass in the roughly hewn portholes he calls windows, so could he therefore shut up and climb through one of them instead of waking up the whole road. He told me to mind my own business and called me a 'wise guy', which was rich coming from a man wearing no shoes and a black and orange dress.

Still, at least Fred Flintstone's nightly farce drowns out Tom and Barbara Good's chickens on the other side. And their sty of grunting pigs. And Geraldine their goat (to whom I was once formally introduced) endlessly doing whatever it is that a goat does, at maximum volume. I heard braying the other day and thought that they'd added a donkey to their collection. Then I realised it was the Leadbetters, next-door-but-one, having one of their Conservative Club meetings. I never realised livestock could be so noisy. Even livestock with names. The only time they're quiet is when they're defecating.

I must say, recently I've been sorely tempted to set the Flintstones' monstrous cat on the lot of them – one of those chic new crossbreeds with fangs – but Elizabeth, my wife, told me I was being irrational. And anyway, they're just as bad with their menagerie of animal slaves. It's enough to make you want to call the RSPCA. When Lenin, the Goods' cockerel, escaped from his coop they eventually found him in the Flintstones' living room. He'd been used as a record player for three days. I think Tom was secretly quite impressed. That was when the Goods had started playing music to their vegetables to help them grow, and that evening I saw him and Barbara swearing loudly as they wrestled with a hen and a wind-up gramophone.

After that, Tom started 'popping over' to see if he could pick up any tips from Wilma about animal husbandry (and I don't mean Fred). I'd hear them chatting in the Flintstones' rock-strewn garden among the palms, him in his scabby dark green jumper, her, as ever, in that spotless white dress, whatever the weather. He'd ask about how they managed to get a small mammoth to be a vacuum cleaner, or how a bee in a clam could be used as a shaver. And she'd always say, 'Ask Fred.' He even enquired about that wooden steamroller-car of theirs. It goes like the clappers but runs on nothing, which is why Good was so keen. He's already built a generator in their basement that chugs like a Model T and runs on animal dung. What next? A car that runs on urine?

And he'd always go round when the overbearing Fred was out at work. I don't blame him. I remember when that loudmouth first moved in. He'd bound up to me and bellow, 'Put it there, Reggie boy', whenever he saw me.

Then he'd start telling me what it was like to live in the 'oldest property in town', calling it 'an original'. Well, it's certainly that. The Leadbetters apparently refer to it as a 'gothic stone folly'. They would. I just call it an eyesore.

Strangely, none of this ever seems to bother my wife Elizabeth. Whenever I bring it up she just gives me one of her anodyne smiles and tells me that I need a holiday. She's probably right. But I'd only come back to the same neighbours. The Bohemian buffoon on one side and the grow-your-own, self-sufficiency nuts with their shambles of a garden on the other. Honestly, it's like a tramp's allotment with its wire fences and maze of duckboards.

Although you can at least talk to Tom and Barbara. I shared some dreadful homemade wine with Tom once. He offered it up as an apology when one of their pigs dug beneath the fence and laid waste to Elizabeth's petunias. 'Peapod Burgundy?' he said, handing me a ropey-looking bottle. Its kick was worse than Geraldine's. After a couple of glasses (the flowerbeds got most of mine, killing even more of the petunias), he pointed to his garden and said it was the future, and that in thirty years' time all mod cons would be just that: cons. I thought he was mad.

But then, this morning, I looked out at him and Barbara, toiling away beneath the cold grey skies, at odds with the suburban world of twitching nets and crazy paving. And I realised there was something about their naïve and slightly smug endeavour, somewhere between heroic and desperate, that touched me. Poor fools. It must be hard. Apparently, they've started swapping turnips for newspapers down at the tobacconist. And last week the window cleaner told me that Barbara offered him 'a bottle of homemade wine, half a dozen lettuces and a pound of spring onions', instead of his usual five pounds.

Elizabeth says I'm imagining all of it, of course. Every night, when I complain about Flintstone yelling and tell her that I'd like to put those clucking chickens in a Kiev, she tells me that I've left the television on downstairs again. 'You know, I really think you need to sort this out,' she says, with one of her smiles. And she's right, I do. And I will. I can see the headline in the local paper now: Senior Sales Executive, Reginald Perrin, 46, Takes Life In Hand Shock. I can't wait.

How Listings Magazines (Almost) Tore My Family Apart – Ian Jones

Certain things were not welcome in my house when I was growing up. Top of the list was Labour Party election literature. Second was swearing. And third was the *TV Times*.

My parents weren't puritans, the sort who only give sticks and satsumas on Christmas Day. I think they were both keen to bring me and my sister up on their own terms and not those of their respective parents. But why the prejudice against a listings magazine? After all, my mum and dad did watch ITV. They must have. To be honest, before I reached the age of ten I can't recall them switching over to it in my presence, but I'm pretty sure they weren't averse to the occasional half-hour with *George and Mildred* or, at a push, high tea with the toffs of Brideshead. But for them the BBC was the default choice. It was always Auntie's news rather than ITN in our house. Come Saturday nights, it was BBC1 all the way, from *The Generation Game* to *Match of the Day*.

Totem of their love for the corporation was *Radio Times*, which, unlike its rival, was bought religiously every week. Naturally I fell in love with it, über-sticky over-colourised jagged-edged pages and all. It gave me as much primary-school nourishment as any amount of Curly Wurlys, and I spent more than one summer holiday cutting up back issues and reassembling them according to my own demented fantasy schedule.

The one occasion the *TV Times* was allowed across the threshold, however, was in the last week of December. The sight of that festive double issue resting close to our black-and-white Grundig set, usually with Bet Lynch or Princess Diana on the front cover, meant the holiday season had truly begun. It was a bit like the raising of the *Mary Rose*: a historic behemoth suddenly back in public view, its innards promising treasures.

For those two weeks I revelled in the *TV Times*, knowing I would not have such unfettered access to the inside scoop on *Family Fortunes* or *Rainbow* for another year. At least, not under my own roof. For there was one place I could peruse the magazine any time I chose: and that was my grandparents' house. Here was a very different world indeed; one of framed prints of Constable's *The Hay Wain*, endless barley sugars and . . . ITV! *All day long!* I relished the chance to stay with my grandparents, though not, if I'm being brutally honest, out of familial affection. Oh no. I went there for non-stop Anne Diamond, Ted Rogers and Alastair Burnet. And the copy of *TV Times* on the coffee table.

This dichotomy was never discussed. And I could never, ever introduce contraband from one territory to the other. No, it was a fully-fledged inter-generational listings war. A copy of *Radio Times* on my gran's sideboard? *The shame of it!* Attempting to slip an edition of *TV Times* into my mum's shopping trolley, meanwhile, resulted in the silent treatment all the way home.

Only later, when I was older and claiming the right to watch what I wanted when I wanted, did I figure out what was going on. There was a taboo surrounding ITV among folk of my parents' age. It was a channel to be tolerated but rarely enjoyed. For folk my grandparents' age, however, it was a channel that brought solace and salvation.

They were the people who had been adults at the time of its birth in 1955, back when the BBC was a starch-shirted dunderhead who didn't understand what television was for. Perhaps my grandparents bought their first set just so they could see ITV. They certainly treasured the channel, maybe more for what it was once was than what, by the early 1980s, it was starting to become: less the buccaneer, more the bank clerk. But they had grown up and grown old with it; they weren't going to give up on it now. And my parents' generation had, as they had with almost everything else, set their minds against what their own mum and dad had reared them upon. Out went Hughie Green and Noele Gordon, in came Frank Bough and Esther Rantzen.

I thought I had it sussed. What narrow-minded fools my mum and dad were! They'd merely exchanged one prejudice for another. Come my early teens, however, I'd shunned both the BBC *and* ITV and was planting my flag exclusively in Channel 4, dazzled by the appeal of *Whose Line Is It Anyway?* and *The Wonder Years*. I was startled to find their attitudes had rubbed off on me. It was the ultimate humiliation for a fourteen-year-old: to discover yourself behaving exactly like your own parents.

A few years later the listings war was over, and magazines won the right to print information on whatever channels they liked. My mum and dad continued buying *Radio Times*, but slowly their habits changed. I watched them become channel hoppers. Scruples mellowed, dogma melted. Fast forward to the twenty-first century. And, yes, I still buy *Radio Times*, and only *Radio Times*, despite a multitude of alternative listings guides in print and online. Bonds forged in battle run deep, and I feel I owe the magazine, if not my love, then at least my loyalty. I suspect this is a lifetime's commitment. I also suspect it's one that puts me in a minority of less than two . . .

6

Chucklevision:
The Serious World of Comedy

In which comedies feel the heat and keep repeating on us, Nicholas Lyndhurst fails to be Sam Tyler and canned laughter gets canned.

Dead parrots, pirate memory games, suits-you-sirs, how I love comedy sketches set in shops. For any connoisseur of the format I'd like to recommend two classics: Victoria Wood's *Shoe Shop Sketch* and Fry and Laurie's *The Hedge Sketch*.

Quite why Julie Walters prowling towards Victoria Wood in a shoe shop declaring 'We think we've got hens in the skirting board' is so funny could be down to any number of things: the unexpected surrealism in such a banal setting; 'hens' is genius – if you'd never seen the sketch before there is absolutely no way you would ever guess that was coming; the violent and manic performance from Walters, snapping the heels off of a pair of stilettos in response to Wood's desire for flat shoes – 'flatter now' she leers, frighteningly; the relentless barrage of jokes in Victoria Wood's script never giving you a second to catch your breath; and the setting itself – sketches set in shops are cosy, familiar and usually signal that you're in for a classic. Anyone who thinks Victoria Wood's comedy is all about subtle human observation should watch this: it's every bit as insane as Tubbs and Edward in their Local Shop and surprising as Ronnie Barker's shopping list when he asks whether Ronnie Corbett has got any 'o's. Recently Little Miss Jocelyn has been carrying the torch for over-the-counter psychosis with her amazing library sketch, playing the middle-class woman who throws a violent, ear-splitting toddler tantrum when someone else gets the book she wants. It's properly, brilliantly terrifying.

The Hedge Sketch sees Fry as shopkeeper and Laurie as customer attempting to buy a hedge in what would be the unfunniest shop sketch ever, if it weren't for the moment where Laurie manages to skip his line and the two men find they have swapped characters halfway through. Rather like the characters in Michael Frayn's *Noises Off*, where what should be a straightforward farce falls to bits around the actors, the fun in *The Hedge Sketch* comes from the look of panic on the actors' faces as they realise their predicament, and their desperate attempts to seam-lessly solve their problem and get back on track without the audience noticing.

When we first got a video recorder in 1983 I recorded several episodes of an ITV sitcom and became complete-ly obsessed with watching them over and over again. It's clear to me that *Brass* should be as celebrated as that other brilliant historical sitcom from the eighties, *Blackadder*. It was a spoof of clogs and shawls dramas in the style of *Dallas*, but what I only half-grasped at the time was that it was full of other parodies too: of *Lady Chatterley's Lover*, *Maurice*, numerous Bernard Shaw and Oscar Wilde plays, Merchant Ivory films and *Brideshead Revisited*. It's *Airplane!* does Penguin Modern Classics.

I mention *Airplane!* because it's full of terrible 'don't call me Shirley' jokes and alarmingly OTT acting. One moment Agnes Fairchild was throwing herself across tables sobbing *Jaaaaack!,* the next she'd be unbuttoning her heaving cleavage and growling like a tigress in heat. Morris was a gloriously camp and lascivious cross between Sebastian Flyte and Uncle Monty from *Withnail and I.* And the monstrous Lady Patience added a *Dynasty*-style dash of super-bitch, wheeling herself about in her bath chair, spooning gin from a soup bowl and plotting to have her husband blown up by her manic son Austin. As a child I watched it over thirty times, and it never stopped being funny – and just a little bit sexy. Though, like Larry Grayson's oft-mentioned friend Everard, it's much filthier than I realised at the time.

My obsession for *Brass* was only equalled when *Spaced* was finally released on DVD and I could spend weekends listening to Officially The Best Commentary Track Of All Time and discussing with my flatmate which one of us was Tim and which was Daisy (although as with Tim and Daisy's mistaken belief that they would be Fred and Daphne in *Scooby Doo*, we were probably more like Mike and Marsha).

It's easy to get nostalgic about comedy shows from the 'golden age' but happily the sitcom seems to have staged a bit of a resurgence on the margins of the schedules. BBC3 deserves a lot of credit for trying out new voices amongst the seemingly endless dross they put out, and because of that we have the sublime *The Inbetweeners*. Then there's the inexplicably cancelled *Pulling*, the dark and outrageous sitcom following the lives of three women turning thirty and unable to settle down, told with something of the amoral cruelty of *The Sarah Silverman Show* and *Nighty Night*. And one of the stars from from *Pulling*, Rebekah Staton, has turned up in ITV2's surprisingly good first-ever commissioned sitcom *No Heroics*, set in a bar for superheroes; imagine *Cheers* crossed with *Heroes*. Well, it's nothing like that. *The IT Crowd* is the best kind of nonsense, not trying to be clever, just being relentlessly silly. On paper, *Flight of the Conchords* sounds like the worst idea ever – a sitcom with songs! – but their hang-dog performances and the small cast of brilliant minor characters has made this into a bit of a classic. And *Outnumbered* has confounded all expectations about what a mainstream sitcom on BBC1 can be like these days: basically, not focus-grouped to shit. And with actual jokes. With Karen we see the birth of a TV comedy legend, whose mini-Margo-style diatribes are all the more remarkable for the fact that the show is partly improvised and she's only about seven years old. The future's bright. The future's Karen.

Top Ten Comedies – Boyd Hilton

Hello my name is Boyd and I'm a *Frasier*-holic.

I must have watched every episode of the *Cheers* spin-off at least a dozen times. And there are 264 of them. Yet every now and then on a Saturday morning as I'm flicking through the digital channels, conjuring up displacement activities in lieu of tidying my flat and, heaven forbid, doing some Dyson-ing, I still get overly excited when I see that the Paramount Comedy channel is having yet another *Frasier* Weekend. This means I can sit there, quaff coffee and relax whilst watching six, ten, maybe even twelve episodes of *Frasier* in a row. All over again.

For me, such repeat watchability is unique to comedies. I know there are many intelligent, discerning people out there who enjoy sitting through the same episodes of *Star Trek* and *Doctor Who* again and again, memorising each line of dialogue whilst enduring accusations of nerdism and geekery from their loved ones. But one or two viewings of even the very best sci-fi episode or serial drama is enough for me. I'm a comedy dweeb and proud of it. Or at least not ashamed of it. And there are thousands of us out there. Pretty much every major comedy writer and performer you've ever heard of is a total comedy nerdling too. Ricky Gervais can discuss *The Simpsons* for hours on end. Matt Lucas has an encyclopaedic knowledge of everything Vic and Bob have ever done. Rob Brydon can analyse *Seinfeld* till the cows come home. And seemingly ever major A-list American comedian is obsessed with the original UK version of *The Office*.

I mention all this by way of explanation for the list that

follows. It's an entirely personal selection of the ten best TV sitcoms of all time. Yet it is scientific. The infallible measure I've used is to work out on a piece of paper which shows I most readily and happily re-watch either on DVD or digital TV. And let's face it you can pretty much get anything on DVD these days, from *The Phil Silvers Show* to bloody *Two Pints of Lager*. (Sorry for mentioning those in the same sentence.) Actually, there is one classic US show in my Top Ten which outrageously isn't available on DVD at time of writing and nor is it frequently repeated on UK TV. It might be fun to see if you can spot it. Clue: the title rhymes with Yoda.

Finally let me just say, yes this is an indulgently personal list. Yes, I've unbelievably left off some cast-iron classics (*The Simpsons, The Larry Sanders Show, Reginald Perrin* come to mind) and some huge popular hits (*Only Fools and Horses, Friends, One Foot in the Grave, Cheers, M*A*S*H* . . .). All I can do is apologise and go back to my overriding criterion. This is simply a list of the TV comedies to which I am most addicted, in order of addictiveness, accompanied by some vague attempt to explain why. Feel free to throw your hands up in horror at my failure to include *Last of the Summer Wine*. Seriously, what was I thinking?

1 *The Office*

Number one? Really? Yes, I know it's barely a few years old, and there are only 13 episodes, but *The Office* is the show which seems to reveal more wonders every time I watch it. Every nervous pause, every smooth of the tie, every shot of the photocopier sorting through paper, all of it, is simply perfect. Yet somehow it seems to get even better, even funnier, even more emotionally satisfying, with each viewing. It also warms my heart's deepest cockles that such a brilliant piece of TV actually became an enormous popular phenomenon around the world. We all know who David Brent is, and I think we always will.

2 *Seinfeld*

American sitcoms never cease to amaze me. I know they have gazillions of Ivy League-educated writers paid vast amounts to work all hours. But it's still remarkable how that system can produce hundreds of beautifully wrought comedy gems. It's like the best, most unfeasibly creative factory in the world. And Seinfeld must be the system's most daring, uncompromising and *funny* product of all. It's basically New York Jewish humour and neurosis turned into a number one primetime comedy which dared to have an episode built round a masturbation competition and failed to provide for its characters any kind of personal growth. The secret of its success? Maybe it's just that we all like to imagine we have friendships as effortlessly engaging and entertaining as those of Jerry, George, Elaine and Kramer?

3 *Frasier*

I've gone for Frasier rather than *Cheers*, even though *Cheers* was first and was itself routinely wonderful. But *Frasier* is surely the most miraculously clever, sophisticated, witty sitcom to ever hit the top of the ratings. It also has the best ensemble of supporting characters (ultra-flamboyant yet happily married restaurant critic Gil Chesterton might just be my favourite thing about the whole series). The best episodes (I'm thinking of the likes of 'Ham Radio', in which Frasier tries to re-create a fifties-style radio murder mystery) have a giddy appreciation of the joys of farce. And no, it was never quite the same once Niles got together with Daphne, but even in its later years, Frasier was still capable of great comedic heights.

4 *Curb Your Enthusiasm*

Everyone in the TV comedy world loves *Curb* to such an extent, it's become a cliché. But the reason they all love it is because it is so unwaveringly good. Weirdly, it's often described as being 'dark' yet it's literally sunny, taking place mostly in LA, and Larry himself is having a great time hating everyone and everything. Even when it deals with death, terminal illness, disability and all those traditionally dark subjects, it does so with an almost gleeful sense of fun. Debate rages among *Curb* fans about how the six seasons so far compare. I'm just happy to randomly shove any of them in my DVD player and bathe in the sheer joy of Larry and manager Jeff bantering away to their hearts' content.

5 *Fawlty Towers*

Some TV shows can become tired merely due to over-exposure. *Fawlty Towers* is regularly voted the best sitcom ever, it's been repeated regularly since it first aired in the mid-seventies, and it's still on every other week on some UK 'gold' channel or other, yet whenever I do find myself accidentally tuning in, I invariably get hooked. Amazingly, unbelievably, it hasn't really dated. Okay, the sets are palpably rickety and some of the jokes are politically incorrect, but the stories are so brilliantly constructed, the characters so well observed and performed, that its qualities seem truly timeless. *Fawlty Towers* is the ultimate proof of the enduring power of classic TV comedy.

6 *The Royle Family*

Before *The Office* made comedic ultra-realism fashionable, there was Caroline Aherne and Craig Cash's real-time, one-set masterpiece mostly about a family just watching the telly. The BBC originally wanted it to be a traditional studio-based sitcom, complete with laughter track. But Aherne stood firm. How right she was. Each episode of *The Royle Family* is like a half-hour Mike Leigh film or Alan Bennett play. Except funnier and warmer. And more real.

7 *I'm Alan Partridge*

Series two of *I'm Alan Partridge* might be the most criminally under-rated TV comedy of all. How can any series that featured Norwich DJ Partridge's vivid mime re-enactment of the opening of *The Spy Who Loved Me* or his plaintive cry of 'Dan! Dan! Dan! Dan! Dan! Dan! Dan! Dan! Dan! Dan! Dan!' when he spots his new best friend Dan in the distance, ever have received such middling reviews? Steve Coogan's sheer joy at being able to play such a delicious character shines through in every scene. And let's not forget this is the show which coined the immortal phrase 'Monkey Tennis'.

8 *Ever Decreasing Circles*

John Esmonde and Bob Larbey are best known for their four gloriously enjoyable series of *The Good Life*. Yet for me their greatest achievement is the hugely under-valued *Ever Decreasing Circles*. *EDC*, as I've suddenly decided to call it, stars *The Good Life*'s remarkable Richard Briers as a particularly annoying, small-minded suburbanite who possibly suffers from some kind of obsessive-compulsive disorder, but no one knew what that was in 1984. *Circles*, as I'm now calling it, also featured the best put-upon-wife character in sitcom history – Ann, as played by Penelope Wilton, was wise, sexy, tolerant and ever-so-subtly aware of being trapped in a life with a bit of a loser. And let's not forget Howard and Hilda, in their matching cardigans, two of the finest, most lovable comedy creations ever to grace our screens. *Ever Decreasing Circles* regularly reached levels of profundity and pathos only hinted at by most earnest dramas.

9 *Rhoda*

This is the most personal choice of my Top Ten. I was pretty much brought up on *Rhoda*, and along with the early, funny films of Woody Allen, it shaped my sense of humour. Such as it is. In fact, *Rhoda* was pretty much like a weekly Woody Allen film, full of unvarnished New York Jewish humour – with lots of sarcasm, self-deprecation (especially from Rhoda's sister Brenda, played by Julie Kavner, aka Marge Simpson) and an obsession with overbearing mothers. Rhoda herself was just your typical insecure Jewish girl. But she was so funny and lovable she topped the US ratings, just like that other Jewish New Yorker, Jerry Seinfeld. One day it'll come out on DVD or Blu-Ray or whatever and everyone can remember what a classic show *Rhoda* was.

I was torn for the tenth position in my highly prestigious list between the meticulously crafted, very British brilliance of *Yes Minister* and the ramshackle edginess of *The Larry Sanders Show*. In the end it came down to this: I haven't seen an episode of *Sanders* for a couple of years, and weirdly I don't miss it. Yet I still regularly watch *Yes Minister*, with Paul Eddington's fabulously vain, clumsy politician Jim Hacker clashing with his witheringly imperious civil servant Humphrey (Nigel Hawthorne). There isn't a scene wasted in the entire five series.

I Was a *TV Burp* Script Associate
– David Quantick

I have the best job in the world. It's also the worst job in the world. I work on the television series *Harry Hill's TV Burp*. My job is to watch tapes of next week's television and think of jokes about it. It is a job which makes some people envious. To them, watching endless hours of *EastEnders* and *The Bill* and *The X Factor* is heaven. They're wrong. It is a mind-numbing burning horror which surely was devised by Satan to torment his most evil clients. 'Ah, Saddam Hussein, welcome to hell – here's your six-hour tape of *Emmerdale*, enjoy.' Yes, that's what the Devil would say.

It is the best job as well, though, because unlike those poor hypothetical inmates of hell, I do at least get my own back. My colleagues – Dan, Brenda, Paul and of course Harry himself – are lucky in that we are permitted on television – on the actual medium we are mocking – to not so much bite the hand that feeds us as chew it off and write on it in red ink HA HA LOOK I BIT YOUR HAND OFF CAN I HAVE ANOTHER ONE PLEASE? And we do it in front of seven million people, which is also nice.

Television now is a strange thing. Once there were so few channels that there was lots and lots of money to go round. Between the BBC's licence fee (since you're asking, the single best invention of the twentieth century) and ITV's advertisers, the dosh was flowing in, and many, many television programmes had extremely decent production values, acting, scripts and themes. It wasn't all *The Singing Detective*, true, but it was a world where even soap operas could be great. (If you don't believe that last statement, look at any article about *Coronation Street* written before about 1985. The show then was a mixture of genuinely funny sitcom, brilliant character writing and even some gentle social comment. Now? At best it's mildly entertaining, at worst it's some idiot's idea of how Alan Bennett thinks poor people talk.)

These days, we have many, many channels. The BBC has been remodelled as a half-arsed sort of commercial station, like a hospital forced to 'outsource' and other ludicrous nineties jargonology. And there isn't any money. As a result, television shows are cheaply made, but in ludicrous ways. Money isn't everything; in radio, having limitations has produced fantastic shows. In telly, however, lack of money means lack of anything. And since the invention of reality TV – stop me if you've heard this – actors and proper scripted narrative are out the window, too.

Worst of all is the bread that goes into the televisual sausage. Once upon a time if a show was bad, at least it was short. Twenty-three minutes on ITV, thirty on BBC. But now thin ideas are spread out for an entire hour. Documentaries go on for days. You start to notice the tricks: the incessant repeating of shots, the endless summing-up of what we've just seen, the inclusion of footage where nothing happens (things like phone calls to people who are out), and worst of all, the dread words 'coming up'. Once upon a time the phrase 'coming up' would only be followed by the words 'in part two'. Now they just chuck it in the middle of a show to kill time. It's in shows with no part two. They just say it. Soon we'll be doing it at home. 'Coming up – who'd like a cup of tea?'

All this is at least good for those of us at *TV Burp*. Take a show like *EastEnders* – a programme so awful, so grim and so inept that it took the character of the cheery Cockney and turned it into a bleak, child-molesting, neighbour-murdering, humourless freak. *EastEnders* is made so quickly, written so badly, and acted so weakly that there's lots to take the mickey out of there. Look at one of the many vain action-hero documentaries out there, where men claiming to be survival experts spend slightly too much time with their trousers off in the Arctic. These shows are lightbulbs of vanity, and these characters – the replacements for the real explorers and frontier-crossers of old – are just asking to be mocked.

So I work for *TV Burp* (my official title is script associate, which is very nice). It is the worst job in the world, and it is the best job in the world. And that will do me nicely.

Gary Sparrow's Paucity of Ambition
– Richard Herring

When it first aired in the 1990s I dismissed *Goodnight Sweetheart* as a rather run-of-the-mill, traditional sitcom, albeit with the unusual premise that its protagonist was able to time-travel between the nineties and the forties. Having recently rewatched pretty much every one of the fifty-eight episodes on its daytime daily repeat on ITV3 (slightly discombobulated by the fact that this BBC series is having a bigamous relationship across the decades with another channel), I have now decided that my initial, casual analysis of the programme was pretty much on the button. Yet there are occasions when it transcends its sitcom bounds to examine the interesting philosophical, ethical and temporal conundrums of the situation and I can't help thinking it was a bit of a missed opportunity.

It could have been the *Life on Mars* of the nineties, but due to its general lightness of touch, both in the writing and the acting, it is a disappointment. A disappointment, however, that I am becoming increasingly obsessed about, partly because I believe it is crying out for a remake. Why not? There have been many, many brilliant sitcoms turned, years later, into disappointing films. Why not a disappointing sitcom turned into a brilliant film (or TV comedy drama).

Ironically I wish that I had some kind of time portal back to the early 1990s so I could wrestle this idea from the hands of creators Marks and Gran, and maybe also have a secret affair with the young Dervla Kirwan – though not her replacement for the last three series, Elizabeth Carling. Both of Sparrow's wives were recast after series three, at which point I would switch allegiances to the new Yvonne Sparrow, Emma Amos. It's not just the temporal paradoxes that are confusing.

For those of you less au fait with the *Goodnight Sweetheart* canon, the series revolves around TV repairman, Gary Sparrow (Nicholas Lyndhurst) who discovers a time portal that allows him (and usually only him) to travel between nineties East London and forties East London. Interestingly and unusually for time-travel adventures, the two timelines run concurrently. So if Sparrow spends a day in wartorn London then a day has passed back in the future. He meets the barmaid of the nearest pub to the rift in time and begins to date her, pretending that he works for the secret services. He also impresses the gullible people of the past by passing off popular future hits as his own compositions. He is assisted in the 1990s by his longsuffering friend, Ron, who prints up wartime money for him and helps conceal the bigamy and has his loyalty totally abused by the selfish and duplicitous Sparrow.

Sparrow is in many ways a confused, selfish and unlikeable man. Yet Nicholas Lyndhurst is hopelessly miscast in the role and flounders around, limited to expressions of bafflement and slight moral discomfort, but never convincing that he would be capable of such deceit, unable to convey the complexity of the emotional and moral choices the character must make and unbelievable as an irresistible ladies' man.

Lyndhurst is not helped by the script: we see few of the psychological effects of such a massive lie. Is he struggling with his mendacity and his petty thievery between time zones, or is he in fact liberated by the knowledge

160

that his bigamy will never be discovered because his wives can actually never meet (though of course, as you doubtless recall, they do meet on one occasion when the rift in time is damaged by a bomb)? Is infidelity only a burden because the cheat is always terrified he might be discovered, or would he still feel dead inside? The writers preferred to concentrate on farce, alas.

Frustratingly there is little consistency to the series. For example on one occasion Sparrow influences a tiny event involving Ron's grandad and comes back to find his shop is owned by someone else, his wife has another husband and Ron is, improbably and hilariously, a vicar. Yet a few episodes later, he manages to alter the past so his son will change from a single, childless, alcoholic down-and-out, to a successful businessman with two kids, with no other effects on history.

The thing that amuses me most though is Gary Sparrow's paucity of ambition. He has the opportunity to travel back in time and affect the course of history or at least travel around in the past and what he does instead is just go to the nearest pub to the time portal and get off with the barmaid.

Funnily enough this is slightly addressed in a later episode, where Gary splits into three people, him and a good and an evil version of himself, and the good one mocks him for his lack of scope. Gary is immoral, both by cheating on his wives and recklessly stealing songs and inventions from the future and using them in the past, but he could do so much more: investigate the wartime years more thoroughly, really abuse his powers and become the wealthiest and most influential man in history or at least check out the next pub down the road to see if the barmaid there is any better-looking (certainly in the last three series). But I kind of love Gary Sparrow because of the limitations of his scope. He is an idiot and he's morally dubious, selfish, takes risks with history given what (sometimes) happens when he changes stuff and yet he remains somehow likeable. Maybe Lyndhurst is playing him exactly right after all. As a kind of formless void, unable to really understand the implications of anything he does.

Perhaps I have ended up thinking too much about something which was never intended to stand up to this kind of analysis, and yet I am convinced there is a brilliant comedy science fiction drama waiting to be written, which properly explores what would happen if a TV repairman found a portal that would take him forty-four years into the past. I might just write it myself and then act it out with puppets in my bedroom.

Against Laughter – Bruno Vincent

My pet hate on the telly is only a small thing, so slight in fact that you may not have noticed it, but it annoys me in adverse proportion to the amount of screen time it takes up. Because it'll need a name if I'm to rant about it, I'll call it the Unearned Laugh.

To explain what it is, just picture an advert on prime time telly. One where, instead of just explaining the product (detergent, say), the advert instead gives you a mini drama featuring the sort of archetypal Everyfamily at whom the product is marketed. There's some kind of situation or argument (a child has got ice-cream on its jumper while in the care of its careless and incompetent father) followed by some kind of joke or pay-off, and then it ends, probably with the dad mugging gormlessly in the background as mum solves the problem. At the conclusion of the advert the product, logo and catchphrase appear, of course. But then, just then, in the last hemi-demi-second before the ad disappears, quite often there will be a little giggle.

That's the first type – something totally unfunny followed a few seconds later by an annoying laugh. In this instance the laugh is like a little Microsoft noise to say an email's arrived. 'Joke!' it moronically signals. 'One unopened laugh!' Have you noticed it? If not, you'll have to take my word that it's there, because it is.

The second type of Unearned Laugh is maybe a bit higher in the annoying/insulting stakes. It's the sort of thing Jamie's flatmates would have done in the ads he used to do, and those preppy Doritos friends from a few years back did it all the time. In an ad for a Maltesers, or

Heat, for instance, it might happen like this: in an office environment two women make a vaguely bitchy remark about another woman who walks past in an unflattering top. Then it jump-cuts to them a few seconds later, both bent over with semi-hysterical laughter. Do you see what I mean now? It's as though in some longer version or director's cut of the advert, the dialogue led up to a genuinely hilarious line which was later cut out. What was the missing gag? Will we always be deprived of the genius of those office girls? Will they forever be refused their chance to shine?

This second type is a way of showing a situation that is funny while hiding what's actually funny about it, and as a fan of comedy it seems to me like a really pathetic cheat, like a kind of comedy tax evasion. Worse than that, I'm sure it works on lots of people too, and that marketers might have revealed that the sight of laughter provokes the same positive associations as something actually funny (or something like that). I disagree: if you walk into a pub and see a table of people laughing uproariously at something that happened outside of your earshot, do you think, 'Look at those life-loving young things, I'm kind of jealous of what it is they share'? No, you think: 'Dicks.'

It may be that in some cases (if it's a child's laughter, for instance) it's supposed to convey the fact that the characters are just having fun, rather than actually laughing at something funny. Fair enough. But most of the time the Unearned Laugh is a dirty cheat.

When it comes to comedy and fake laughter, we've put up with canned laughter for decades, and have been immune to it for almost as long (although it's going out of fashion – the best British comedies of the last ten years haven't bothered with it: *Brass Eye, Spaced, The Royle Family, The Office* and others). But at least canned laughter is the sound of a real audience genuinely laughing – mostly it's at the same show which you are watching, albeit they may be laughing at an earlier take of the same joke.

The Unearned Laugh is worse than canned laughter – it's an actor pretending to laugh, for starters. It's also patronising, as though you wouldn't know the ad was supposed to be humorous without them pointing it out (most of these ads, that I have noticed, are aimed at women, which means advertisers think women are humourless, or – more likely – that advertisers are completely humourless themselves). And it's disingenuous and insulting of them to pretend that their ad is funny enough to warrant laughter, which almost completely without exception, they're not. It's also unconfident, as though they're not sure the ad is good enough to be funny of its own accord and they have to point it out. Also, it's counter-productive, because the ads themselves being unfunny, the people in them who are laughing seem horribly smug, or stupid, or maniacal, thus alienating the sensible viewer from the advertised product.

Advertisers: we're British, we've got a pretty good sense of humour, thanks. Don't try to pretend something's funny when it's not. And you don't need to tell us when there's a joke there, we can tell for ourselves whether something's funny. So give it a rest. Or, preferably, just bugger off.

7

What are . . . *feelings*?:
The Illogical World of Cult TV

In which a notable list of celebs fail to get their doctorate, Wonder Woman and Sapphire slug it out and Michael Knight is magnificent.

I once saw Russell T. Davies do a Q and A at the National Theatre where, discussing the reboot of *Doctor Who*, he expressed bafflement at how science fiction is the only genre where you are criticised for writing about human emotions.

Now, I am a massive old-school *Doctor Who* fan. The kind of fan whose hackles rise every time he hears those clichés trotted out about wobbly sets, tinfoil costumes and Daleks not being able to climb stairs. And, sure, actors in the new series may play characters with emotional depth, heartbreaking love stories and tragic fates, but old *Doctor Who* wasn't all twisted ankles and screaming. Forget Rose Tyler or Donna Noble, back then there was a character so resourceful, so lovable, so utterly convincing and well-rounded that my ten-year-old self found an emotional role model for life. Oh K9, my lionheart.

I can't overstate the love I still feel for this remotecontrolled robot dog. When I was a kid I used to imagine how all of my problems would have been solved if I had a K9 of my own: a cute, brainy and occasionally sarcastic robot who could kill people with his nose laser. I'm still to be convinced otherwise. I have the occasional fantasy about us becoming a kick-ass crime-fighting duo, or at the very least taking him on the bus to work and letting him zap people who play music through the loudspeakers of their mobile phones. And, sure, Russell T. used a grown man's love for this very robot dog in *Queer as Folk* as a symbol of his emotional immaturity, but I'm not that easily discouraged. As an ageing *Doctor Who* fan I know all there is about weathering other people's disappointment: after all, I even kept the candle burning through the dark days of Kate O'Mara's stint as The Rani. You have no idea of the tears I cried when K9 left *Doctor Who*. I had my letter read out about it on *Points of View* and everything. I even admit to that. Proudly. Ridicule is nothing to be scared of.

Star Trek is a bit rubbish at emotion, the scriptwriters thinking that it's something they can confine to the holodeck. This is because the setup of *Star Trek* excludes emotion: the *Enterprise* is a corporate office block floating through space and the characters never change out of uniform or have any sort of private lives other than what seem to be extended tea-breaks and water-cooler moments. The typical Spock/Data (and Haddaway) question, 'What is love?', is greeted by the other characters with condescension and a shaking of heads. Like any of the rest of the crew would know – they're too busy being galactic HR to have feelings.

You'd have thought the *X-Files* would have been one of the more emotionally functional cult programmes, given the talent of the two lead actors, but Mulder and Scully had to settle for being absurdly sexy rather than touchy-feely (though, like Phil and Kirstie, their sexiness was both a slow burn and the result of a gradual makeover). It wasn't really till the advent of *Buffy the Vampire Slayer* that cult telly learned to have feelings. And what complex and wonderful feelings they were too; 'I love him but he has no human soul' being a common Dear Deidre problem for our heroine. The death of Buffy's mum is one of the saddest and most emotional moments in cult TV history – the teen show taught the entire genre how to grow up.

And now, along with a newly affecting *Doctor Who* we have *Battlestar Galactica* (the new show so far removed from the first in tone that double-crossing Baltar is no longer some uppity count stuck in Cylon head office with a load of robots, he now has to deal with a slutty lady Cylon who spends most of her time whispering 0898-style sweet nothings with her hands down his shirt) and *Heroes*, which is so intricate and confusing it makes *Lost* look like *Hole in the Wall*. Just don't mention the first two series of *Torchwood*, which despite its best efforts had all of the charm and warmth of a bucket of cold sick. It didn't help that their serious, grown-up base appeared to be the set from a 1986 episode of *Jigsaw*.

Survivors, *Day of the Triffids*, *Doctor Who*, *Battlestar Galactica*, *The Bionic Woman*, *Star Trek* – is there no cult show that is reboot proof? I wonder about SKY bringing back *Blake's Seven*. Looking at the evidence, I suspect Avon and Servalan will be going through a messy divorce, Orac will be a crack whore (Whorac?) and the intergalactic battle between the rebels and the Federation will be relocated to a optician's in Holby. And who knows, it could be all the better for it.

The Doctors Who Weren't – Matthew Sweet

In *Queer as Folk*, Russell T. Davies made a love-test of listing the actors to have played Doctor Who. It was hardly Herculean: when asked the same by Mike Read, at least one smarty-panted viewer of *Saturday Superstore* supplied not just the names of the canonical title-holders (Hartnell, Troughton, Pertwee, etc.) but those of Peter Cushing (who twice fought the Daleks in Cinemascope) and Edmund Warwick, who played the Doctor from behind whenever William Hartnell pulled a sickie. So this is a list from a parallel universe: actors who might have had their moment in front of those roundels, had they not passed on the role – or failed the audition.

The First Doctor

Hugh David was the first man to decline the key to the TARDIS. The invitation was made by Rex Tucker, care-taker producer of the programme when it was still in development. But David had not enjoyed the taste of fame he experienced as the star of Granada's crime series *Knight Errant*, and had no desire to be stared at on buses again. (He returned to the programme as a director, to choreograph the Doctor's tussles with Bonnie Prince Charlie at Culloden and some telepathic seaweed off the coast of Margate.) Verity Lambert, the official first pro-ducer of *Doctor Who*, offered the part to Leslie French, a former dancer who had modelled – in the nude – for the statue of Ariel on Broadcasting House. (He refused, but returned twenty-five years later to play a giggling math-ematician in a Sylvester McCoy story.) Lambert's script editor David Whitaker preferred Cyril Cusack, who was then playing Cassius at Stratford. Geoffrey Bayldon – who later met Tom Baker's Doctor at the bottom of a hole on the planet Chloris – was also considered. William Hartnell got the part.

The Second Doctor

Doctor Who is recast, and it's clear what the production team are after: a character actor with impressive facial crags. Ron Moody said no – and not for the first time. Michael Hordern – a brilliant player who made an entire career from clearing his throat – thumbed his nose at the offer, leaving the field open for Patrick Troughton, another accomplished harrumpher.

The Third Doctor

After Ron Moody had offered his customary rejection, Jon Pertwee persuaded his agent to ring the *Doctor Who* production office to offer his services – only to discover that his name was next on the list.

The Fourth Doctor

For Barry Letts, the producer of Pertwee's run of shows, the spring of 1974 was a series of polite slaps in the face. David Warner did not want to be Doctor Who. Nor did Ron Moody – again. Letts lunched Richard Hearne, a crabbed music-hall turn who had been popular on TV in the 1950s as a character called Mr Pastry – but the actor failed to understand that it was he, and not his alter ego, who was being offered the part, and could not envisage how Mr Pastry would be capable of repelling an alien invasion. Bernard Cribbins came in for an inconclusive cup of coffee. His *Carry On* co-conspirator Jim Dale said he would happily have signed – if he had not already been booked for the rest of the year. The gurgling Scots actor Graham Crowden also said yes – but could not be persuaded to stay for more than one season. (He played a villain in black eyeliner and crow feathers in a story from 1980, and laughed like a skunk during his death scene.) Michael Bentine was mad keen – as were the production team, until they realised that the old Goon was hoping to turn the series into a forum for his ideas about the paranormal. Eventually Fulton McKay – who had kept a seven-foot lizard in his airing cupboard in a story called *Dr Who and the Silurians* – wiggled to the top of the list. Then the BBC's Head of Serials took Letts to see *The Golden Voyage of Sinbad*, a film about a goggle-eyed sorcerer played by a goggle-eyed Liverpudlian named Tom Baker. Baker was working as a hod-carrier on a building site on Ebury Street. Naturally, he said yes.

The Fifth Doctor

Withnail played the Doctor in an animated webcast; 'I' in the 1996 TV movie. In 1980, producer John Nathan-Turner made an unsuccessful attempt to persuade the future Uncle Monty to enter the TARDIS. Richard Griffiths was willing but busy. Then Nathan-Turner's eye was caught by a photograph of Peter Davison. In cricket whites.

The Sixth Doctor

Colin Baker was John Nathan-Turner's first and only choice – but that didn't prevent the *Daily Express* announcing the accession of Brian Blessed.

The Seventh Doctor

For the first time, potential Doctor Whos were auditioned. But not quite for real. Sylvester McCoy was the producer's choice – but to please his bosses, he pointed a video camera at Chris Jury (Lovejoy's adenoidal sidekick), Ken Campbell (who had given McCoy his first gig, banging nails into his nose) and relative unknowns David Fielder and Hugh Futcher.

The Eighth Doctor

A small army of actors were on the producer's wish-list when the first comeback of Doctor Who was planned: Jeremy Brett, Simon Callow, Peter Cook, Jim Dale (again), Michael Gambon, Nigel Hawthorne, Barry Humphries, John Hurt, Derek Jacobi, Herbert Lom, Ian McKellen, Ian McShane, Leo McKern, John Mills, Ron Moody (inevitably), Edward Woodward, Sam Neill, Bob Peck, Donald Pleasance, Jonathan Pryce, Patrick Stewart and Peter Ustinov. Overtures were made to Tim Curry, Hugh Laurie, Griff Rhys-Jones, Eric Idle, Michael Palin, Robert Lindsay, Roger Rees and Rowan Atkinson. Only Lindsay came to audition – and among those who were called to perform a scene between the Doctor and Napoleon Bonaparte were Liam Cunningham, Anthony Head, Rob Heyland, Christopher Bowen, John Sessions, Tony Slattery and Mark McGann. In the end, McGann's brother Paul got the gig – and became exactly what he didn't want to be – 'the George Lazenby of Doctor Whos'.

The Ninth Doctor

He'd already played the part for a *Children in Need*

spoof, but Hugh Grant turned down the chance to take the credit for *Doctor Who*'s whoop-de-do 2005 revival. Does he regret it now, I wonder? Christopher Eccleston's acceptance of the part didn't prevent the *Daily Mail* from declaring Bill Nighy the new Doctor.

Tenth Doctor

David Tennant took the TARDIS unopposed, and by surprise – giving the press no chance to concoct their list of contenders.

Eleventh Doctor

Depressing hotels in London and Cardiff were the venues for top-secret auditions for the new Doctor. For the bookies, Paterson Joseph – star of *Survivors* – had the shortest odds. He certainly read for the part. Nearly seven million viewers tuned into a special programme announcing that complete outsider Matt Smith had been chosen to save the universe each Saturday. New head writer Steven Moffatt swore never to reveal who else was on his shortlist. The Freedom of Information Act will get him in the end . . .

Star-spangled PE Knickers and Fetching Blue Frocks – Bertie Fox

There were two super-powered ladies dominating teatime telly viewing around the turn of the eighties. Wonder Woman arrived on our screens from the US in a technicolour splash of stars, always kitsch, colourful and larger-than-life. Sapphire from *Sapphire and Steel*, meanwhile, was aloof, alien and her motives ultimately baffling.

So there doesn't seem to be much to connect these two characters. One was full of energy, always gallivanting about in the open air, doing those giant springy leaps, and hurling her lasso or tiara in the direction of the nearest Nazi or criminal chump. While the other was prone to skulking in the shadowy corners of lost or abandoned buildings, and could quite easily spend half an hour standing quietly around near a cupboard having a nice think.

But is there more to connect them than we'd think? Women with superhuman abilities wouldn't be so prominent on the TV again for nearly twenty years, so what were the factors that connected these two particular tele-fantasy icons?

Grids and Girdles

More often than not, our first impressions of any leading character on TV come from the show's title sequence. Which means that you'll expect Wonder Woman to be all action, winning smiles, and, well, innovative dress sense, which is fair enough. Sapphire on the other hand – and there's no nice way of saying this – is a little scrunchy ball of blue light emanating from a cosmic grid. So far, so different. But both title sequences share a predilection for crudely-drawn animation (hey, I'm not criticising, I love this stuff!) and improbable pronouncements. The voiceover to *Sapphire and Steel*'s bombastic theme tune left kids everywhere happily baffled with its talk of dimensional irregularities and transuranic heavy elements. And the earnest absurdity of *The New Adventures of Wonder Woman*'s theme's lyrics has never been bettered or, really, equalled. 'In your satin tights, fighting for your rights . . . get us out from under, Wonder Woman!' anyone?

Same Difference

Let's face it, it's hard to identify with either Sapphire or Wonder Woman. Both of them are 'outsiders' to normal humanity, and effectively immortal from our reference point. Sapphire is – well, 'embodiment of an extra-dimensional elemental force' is as good a guess as any – and Wonder Woman is the daughter of the queen of the Amazons, who's spent millennia living on an island idyll far from the world we know. It's interesting that this doesn't tend to happen on TV these days. More recent super-powered women like Buffy the Vampire Slayer and Claire from *Heroes* are ordinary people who have to deal with the consequences of suddenly discovering that they're not like the rest of us. In fact, that becomes one of the main concerns of each of those shows. Were we more able, thirty years ago, to enjoy watching characters who had nothing in common with our own lives?

Shades of Blue

There's no chance of finding any common ground in the field of morality though. Wonder Woman is an old-fashioned girl from a long-standing comics tradition of good guys and bad guys, without shades of grey. But Sapphire is far above such concerns; she appears in our world as a higher being pitted against inexplicable forces to do with Time itself. More often than not, humans are just in the way of that abstracted sort of altercation. On one memorable occasion, which I won't spoil in detail for anyone who's yet to discover this great series, the heart-in-mouth resolution to a long adventure does leave Sapphire appalled at her partner Steel's callous disregard for human life. But a few minutes later she's winsomely sniffing flowers.

Wigs and Wonders

Despite being played by a beauty queen and cavorting merrily through military bases wearing kinky boots and not a great deal else, I don't get the impression that Wonder Woman is supposed to be a sex object. Lynda Carter's performance is so wholesome and big-sisterish that it heads off any such idea. That's part of the charm, as it goes, and those really are PE knickers, after all. Joanna Lumley is much more covered up as Sapphire, in a series of demure blue frocks, the odd fright wig and the occasional bit of brocade.

But excitingly, and crucially, both women have the ability to transform magically into new outfits. Sapphire does it once or twice, mostly to show off, and it's an understated, in-the-twinkle-of-an-eye sort of a thing. But for Wonder Woman, the moment of transformation happened at least once a week and became pretty much the entire point of the show. Well, it was certainly the event I always waited for most eagerly whilst sat in front of her high jinks with a plate of crumpets. Finding a spot where she could be unobserved, dowdy Diana Prince would fling out her arms to the side and begin to twirl around, at which point a glowy ball of light would erupt out of her, filling the screen with an immensely satisfying *THOOOMM!* And when our vision was restored, she'd be there in her skimpy and spangly outfit, hair freshly styled, ready to dash off for more heroics. It was a little intrusion of magic into the everyday world, a trick that she could perform anywhere – even, cunningly, when loosely tied up or falling out of a window – and endlessly repeatable in the playground. Well, if you didn't mind getting beaten up now and again.

Anyway, there was no logical reason for Wonder Woman to spin around to effect her transformation, other than it looked good on the small screen. The burst of light was only introduced by chance to save money, as it got rid of the need for an expensive morphing effect. But as I did set myself the ridiculous task of finding similarities between two such wildly different characters, it's only fair that I save the most tenuous link for my grand 'conclusion'. If a ball of light exploding towards the screen while Wonder Woman spun around was the most iconic thing about her TV incarnation, then is it in any way significant that in the opening titles of *Sapphire and Steel*, we see what you might reasonably assume is Sapphire's true form – and she's spherical, glowing, rushing towards the screen *and* spinning? No? Just me? Ah well.

Behind *Knight Rider*: The Truth Behind the Turboboosts – Christien Haywood

'I wanted to do *The Lone Ranger*, but with a car,' said Glenn A. Larson, series creator of eighties cult hit *Knight Rider*. After crushing thirty-four horses to death trying to get a Trans-Am in the saddle, Larson hit upon a better idea. 'Leave the horses out of it, and just have a man driving a supercar around America. Wearing a mask and shooting Indians.' Following furious protests from the NAACP and pickets outside his studio, Larson had another idea. 'I *don't* want it to be *The Lone Ranger* with a car,' he announced triumphantly, before unveiling his best idea of a man driving a supercar around America who *doesn't* shoot Indians but does solve crimes.

And so, out of that incredibly convoluted brainstorm came one of TV's greatest heroes, Michael Knight, who scoured the highways of America looking for criminals to fight. If the criminals turned out to be Indians, he'd slowly back away and go and look for some other criminals. That was the deal.

The backstory of the show was that Michael, a policeman, had been wounded in the course of duty when a bullet bounced off a metal plate in his head and destroyed his face. This was a real plot idea concocted by real, paid writers. Michael was rescued by billionaire philanthropist Wilton Knight, and given reconstructive surgery so he would look like billionaire philanthropist Wilton Knight so that Michael could go . . . undercover.

I'm proud to announce I've obtained a small scrap of original script from the *Knight Rider* pilot, aired in 1982:

179

Int: Michael Knight comes out of a coma following a horrible shooting.

Wilton: I've given you a new face, Michael – you look just like me!

Michael: Er, yes, great. Um, cheers.

Wilton: So now we look exactly the same!

Michael: . . . Brill.

Wilton: People might get us mixed up! *You* might get us mixed up! You might unzip your trousers, and go 'Hey, is that *my* hand doing that, or Wilton's, cos they look so similar!' Ha ha ha!

Michael begins desperately pressing the 'Call Nurse' button like a demented woodpecker.

Michael gets over this pretty quickly and is told the plan – billionaire Wilton has set up his own high-tech vigilante squad to dish out justice to *'people who operate above the law'* according to the opening titles. Wilton fails to spot the logical flaw in setting up this organisation and away Michael goes. Helping Michael was the other star of the show, KITT, the invulnerable 300mph supercar with a turbocharged heart and the manner of a testy antique shop owner. *'What is it, Michael?'* he'd snap in the middle of a crisis. *'I'm having an English muffin, for God's sake.'* KITT was played by the esteemed character actor William Daniels, who would later go on to play recurring roles in *St Elsewhere* and *Boy Meet World*. For his role in *Knight Rider* Daniels had to wear over 1,110 pounds of prosthetics and stage make-up.

'It was a Knightmare!' he quipped during a Fan Convention in 2007. 'The make-up was so hot and itchy

– and took such a long time to put on! Shooting began at 7 a.m. every day, so you can imagine how early *I* had to get up to start the whole process! We usually started the April before filming.' Despite the difficulties of his craft, Daniels appeared in all eighty-two episodes of *Knight Rider* alongside co-star David Hasselhof, and recalls his time with the actor fondly: 'David was a great guy – really down-to-earth. But so tall! A real big guy – let me tell you, filming the interior scenes with him was a real stretch.' Eventually, due to size constraints, all in-car scenes were shot with Andre the Giant acting as Daniel's body double – with Andre wearing an incredible 2,200 pounds of make-up. Sadly, vicious attacks of agoraphobia and chronic institutionalisation meant that Daniels was unable to shed his prosthetics at the end of the final season. Nevertheless he embarked on a successful career as an actor, which continues to this day. He can currently be seen in the off-Broadway production of Chekhov's *Cherry Orchard*, where he plays a tractor.

Knight's boss and friend in the series was Devon Miles, played by British actor Edward Mulhare. Devon was the starchy-but-fair authority figure who would give Knight his mission for the week, travelling continually in his eighteen-wheel Mobile Command Centre. 'You might recall that KITT always drove up a ramp to get to the Command Centre whilst it was still moving,' recalls Mulhare. 'The truck itself never stopped moving. Some critics thought it symbolised our never-ending war on crime, but actually I was just terrified of parallel parking. I still am!' he chuckles.

Patricia McPherson (who played sassy mechanic Bonnie Barstow) has darker memories of that time, however: 'Devon *was* terrified of parallel parking,' she admits. 'We'd be driving and driving for days, and we'd be pleading with him to pull over, but he'd just scream, "Do you want me *break my wrists*? Is *that* it?" What we didn't know then was a faulty exhaust in the truck meant that poor Edward was suffering from quite severe carbon monoxide poisoning at the time.'

Eventually the show's producers abandoned hopes of Mulhare pulling the truck over, and hit upon the 'rolling Command Centre' idea as a cover up. McPherson picks up the story. 'I spent a total of four years on the truck, filming three seasons of *Knight Rider*. We never stopped once. The Command Centre was featured in three of the four seasons of *Knight Rider*. It should have been all four, but Edward drove the truck to Peru in 1985 and nobody knew where we were.'

Despite the rigours of filming, the crew completed four high-octane series of *Knight Rider* and all remember the experience fondly. 'We weren't just a TV show,' recalls Bea Arthur (the voice of KARR), 'we were a very loving family. All the actors, writers and crew were hugely talented, and it's a testament to that talent that *Knight Rider* is still being viewed today around the world.'

In closing then, perhaps we should give the final word to the show's star, David Hasselhof. Speaking of the huge pool of talent the show drew from, Hasselhof spoke to me personally, via fax from his agent. 'I was magnificent,' he said. 'Simply magnificent.'

8

Carnival of Monsters:
Reality, But Not As We Know It

In which we love the ones we know we should hate, become a top model, rummage through our attics and get judged harshly.

Quick quiz: What are 'Stealth', 'Eclipse', 'Alpha', 'Ignite' and 'Renaissance'? Lose a point if you thought they were *Gladiators*. No, they're faintly ridiculous team names from *The Apprentice*. Although *Gladiators* is half-right because rather than being some kind of business talent academy *The Apprentice* is just an excuse for ludicrous boardroom bitch-fights between extreme cartoon baddies. Dress Phillip and Lorraine in Lycra and give them giant cotton buds and . . . well, that's an image nobody needs really.

Undoubtedly the best episodes of *The Apprentice* are where they go abroad, which they sadly didn't do in 2009. Who can forget Paul and Katie's team in 2007 attempting to sell slabs of plasticky processed cash-and-carry cheese in a farmers' market in France? Or Paul's comeuppance when he refuses to bring his partner in crime, Katie, into the boardroom to answer for their decisions. And then, in 2008 this was topped in Marrakesh in a bartering exercise by what can only be described as the Evil Team, consisting of pathetic loser Michael, Satanic Jenny, Sophie Ellis Bextoid Jennifer, passive-aggressive pouter Alex and Rottweiler Claire. A thrilling series of fuck-ups ensued, from Alex and Claire's hilarious 'role-play' negotiation for a rug, half-Jewish Michael's failure to understand the nature of kosher when buying a chicken and Jenny and Michael's unsuccessful attempt to bribe the employees of a sports shop to sabotage the other team. This led to the best boardroom scene *ever*, taking half of the programme and involving the entire team, resulting in the hugely satisfying firing of both monstrous Jenny and ice-queen Jennifer. As a reality TV programme about business, *The Apprentice* shouldn't be this much fun, but the candidates are brilliantly chosen, every bit as colourful and two-dimensional as their Gladiator counterparts (Courtly Raef! Dotty Lucinda! Insecure Tre! Relentless Saira! Random Jo! And, of course, the Magnificent Churchillian Badger!). With reality TV it's the editing that is the real star. In *The Apprentice* it creates a real sense of drama, transforming their struggles to sell spurious occasion cards to Tesco or apply dodgy photos to cheap mugs into something between high drama and the *Cannonball Run*.

Of course, who wins is largely irrelevant. No one cares which candidate Sir Alan chooses. Push them off a cliff for all we care. No one even cares about the wrinkled Yoda of business, and his colourful turn of phrase (by which I mean the invoking of his arsehole at unexpected moments). It's all about the supporting cast. I want to know more about 'Can-You-Show-Them-In Frances' and her museum-piece Amstrad phone. She may as well be using an Enigma machine. And what does she *do* all day? But most of all I want to see more of Nick and the sadly departed Margaret, waspish and eye-rolling as the gods in *Jason and the Argonauts,* testing us, seeing all and passing judgement with weary sarcasm. Here they are, flanking Sir Alan in a car park, arms folded and posh in the midst of urban decay like a Pet Shop Boys video. There they go, wandering round Marrakesh in shades and it's Noël Coward does *The Matrix.* Unlike the products dreamt up by the candidates, these two are priceless. Will Edinburgh University ever recover from being told it's 'not what it was' by an eye-batting Margaret? Fuck *Hollyoaks Later,* this is the spin-off everyone's after. *Nick and Margaret Unleashed.* Going wild in Monte Carlo and Ibiza, or at the very least, Woking Business Park, arching their eyebrows at each other as they witness our pathetic mortal failings, and being impossibly witty in the bar afterwards as they sip their cocktails.

You only have to have seen streamed footage from the *Big Brother* house to know how critical editing is to the success of reality TV. The live stream was essentially three months' worth of people yawning and wandering round looking for their pants, with the sound of birdsong piped in almost every time they open their stupid mouths and slander someone; the art-house Andy Warhol movie to the edited highlight's show's polished psychodrama. Unlike those of *The Apprentice,* the god of *Big Brother* is invisible, and we are spared the pursed lips and stifled smirks. Instead, this god has lost it over the years. Initially it was sufficient shock for the contestants to discover they would be keeping chickens and using a mangle. Nowadays they are forced to spend days in cardboard boxes or live secret lives within the group. And as the competition has devolved, so have the contestants. They understand what is required of them to a horribly cynical degree. You can see them in the first few minutes in the house sizing each other up to see who is this year's Nadia, Jade, Brian or Ziggy. Most grotesquely the external pressure to play up to their own personas was demonstrated when Nikki was allowed back into the house in Big Brother Seven. After absorbing what it was that made her so popular the person who returned was a *Being John Malkovich* version of herself, a hollow shell steered around the house by an insecure young woman desperately attempting to manufacture moments of spontaneity as 'herself'.

From *Big Brother* there's two directions you can go: towards the hinterland of scheduling, past *Wife Swap* and *Airport* to genuine fly-on-the-wall documentaries such as *The Family* or *Seven Up*; or to the heart of light entertainment, and the spangles, glitter and showbiz pizzazz of *The X-Factor, I'm a Celebrity . . . Get Me Out of Here!* and *Strictly Come Dancing*. I'd happily push the contestants (and judges) of *The X Factor* face-first through a wood-chipping machine. Take that for your tear-jerking stories and desperate vibrato, you cunts. And as for former judge Sharon I-married-a-heavy-metal-star-and-now-I-pretend-I-like-boybands Osbourne and Louis I-secured-my-place-in-hell-when-I-created-Boyzone Walsh, every time I see them I wonder who is taken in by their insincere simpering. I am convinced Walsh drags up to appear as agony aunt Denise Robertson on *This Morning*, who oozes exactly the same level of emotive nonsense and judgemental claptrap as the Irish svengali. Danni Minogue and Cheryl Cole appear to have been manufactured in the same android factory, and Simon Cowell sits there at the end of the desk laughing at the lack of talent of his co-judges and the desperate emotional spew retched up by the contestants.

I am more of a *Strictly* man. When it began here was a perfect piece of Saturday night television, harking back to *The Generation Game*: an expert teaches a no-hoper something complicated and then we either laugh at their failure or applaud their pluck. But what charm it ever had has been lost. Stage-school brats now see it as a great way to kick-start their moribund careers and get them a lead in *Joseph*, and for half of the cast it's hard to tell which are the professional dancers and which are the celebrities.

Now, there was a reason *Come Dancing* was dropped all those years ago – who wants to see lots of orange desperados prancing about competently to bad versions of Randy Crawford songs every week? Pretty it may be, but it's no fun at all. What the amateur dancers bring is entertainment, the spirit of *The Morecambe and Wise Show*. Kate Garraway was Penelope Keith trying to climb down that half-finished staircase and John Sergeant brought back happy memories of Richard Baker running breathlessly about to 'There is Nothing Like a Dame'. The judges (or 'the zhuzzjez' as Tess Daly would have it) are routinely furious as 'serious contenders' are voted out over no-hopers week after week by the public, but stuff the serious contenders, give us more failure to dazzle.

What it really needs is the godlike presence of Margaret and Nick to cast their critical eye on the proceedings and for Margaret to slyly announce that '*Strictly Come Dancing* is not what it was'.

My Irrational Hatred of Reality TV Show Contestants – Emma Kennedy

Let's get one thing straight from the off. I'm a gentle soul: I like to skip through bluebells, I'm not averse to a kitten in a sock and I have been known to help old ladies with beards. I'm a calm and rational woman but when I found myself standing and screaming 'Fuck off! Fuuuuuck Offffff!' at Darius Danesh who had stepped on to stage at the *Pop Idol* concert at Wembley I realised that something in my life had gone terribly, catastrophically wrong. I was in the VIP box spewing blind white hate from the slimy recesses of my gullet, whilst my friend, who had invited me, turned and, with a shock normally reserved for baby killers, said 'Emma! What are you doing? It's only Darius!'

She was right. It was only Darius. And I hated him.

I don't know why and I don't know how but every year since reality TV clamped its icy talons on the nation's psyche I have developed a dangerously violent hatred of at least one participant. Darius, with his rancid ponytail and his constant insistence that he could 'feel the love in the room' was my first, stirring within me a frenzied boiling so intense that if I'd had a pickaxe I would have happily stove his brains in. He popped my irrational cherry and for that, I suppose, he deserves my begrudging thanks but like all newcomers, it was only a matter of time before he was replaced. Darius was to be the tip of the iceberg. There was a behemoth bearing down towards me from which there was no chance of escape.

Big Brother, the Nuclear Warhead of reality television, has blasted our living rooms with housemates like wannabe cluster bombs, leaving a trail of irritating destruction in their wake. When Michelle Bass from *BB* series five sang *Pie Jesu* (pronounced Pii Jeezoo) it was a defining moment. Somewhere, in the deep recesses of my brain, something burst. The synapses responsible for rational thought exploded and I found myself shaking a fist at my television screen. Actually shaking a fist. Like a proper Ol' Timer in raggedy dungarees with a corn pipe hanging off a bottom lip. As Maxwell, the following year, stuck his libidinous tongue out for the hundredth time and slimed that everything was 'off the hook', my eye-balls rotated in their sockets as the red mist of rage descended yet again. In series eight, as tantrum number 357 poured forth from Chanelle, whining about having to eat half a carrot or the devastation of having a natural curl in her hair, I wanted to storm the compound, remove her from the house and drop her into a vat of slow-drying cement. These feelings weren't right. They weren't normal. And yet year on year, up they bubbled until I blew like Krakatoa.

Why do I feel so venomous and hostile towards these people? It's utterly pointless. What do I expect? They're contestants on a reality TV show whose only *raison d'être* is fame at any cost. This is the generation for which nothing has to be earned: instead riches are delivered on a silver platter made from column inches and drunken nights at China Whites. How could I possibly be thrown into a rage by a bunch of idiots whose aspirations are shallower than a saucer made from tissue? The answer, sadly, is because I enjoy it. Where would Peter Pan be without Captain Hook? Harry without Voldemort? They are the ones we love to hate. Every *Big Brother* needs a villain: Makosi, Grace and Charley – all *so* bad they were good again. And the worse you are, the higher the reward. Nobody remembers the nice guys. Rottenness and blind ambition achieve the holy grail of no-hopers everywhere: you'll be etched into the collective memory banks forever. So if you want to be a successful reality-TV contestant there's really only one option. Be as awful as you possibly can be. Lie, cheat, gossip, throw tantrums and glory will be yours. There are five golden rules to follow:

1 Have an opinion of yourself inflated to the point of bursting.
2 Cry. *All* the time. But *only* about important things like smudges or hair straighteners.
3 Speak before you think. Always.
4 As soon as is humanly possible, declare a desire to release a pop single whilst singing 'Umbrella' by Rhianna on a loop. Badly.
5 Possess no talent whatsoever.

Then and only then will a world filled with magazine deals and (whisper it softly) a reality TV show dedicated to you be yours. Who goes? You decide. (As long as it's Darius, preferably taken out and trampled by a herd of overweight, stampeding teenagers). It's what he would have wanted . . .

America's Next Top Model: aka The Last Bitch Standing – Alex Young

This is your handy ten-point guide to winning the USA's most prestigious reality show that isn't *American Idol* . . .

You need an awesome backstory

As is the rule with ongoing reality shows, unless you were taking part in the first series, which featured relatively normal people, one of whom might possibly have had a shot at making it as a model, every contestant must have an 'issue', so they can all go on a 'journey'. Sample 'life challenges' (don't call them problems!) have been: a girl who was going blind; an autistic girl; a butch lesbian; and a girl of Somali origin ('you're *definitely* going to be the next Iman!') who'd been circumcised. Yikes. Usually there's a Bible-basher who freaks out when she's asked to model topless, contrasted with a Mormon who's also been a pole dancer. So, pick an issue/condition and prepare to start crying when anyone asks you about it.

Keep Tyra onside

ANTM is fronted, produced and generally owned by awesome glamazonian Tyra Banks, a woman with a giant melon for a forehead, curves that wax and wane at a weekly rate but certainly wouldn't have afforded her much work in the controversial 'heroin chic' period and a love of gigantic hair in unflattering shades. She's a mix of Oprah-style 'You go, girl!' pep-talk and 'constructive' criticism, big sister (there's an episode near the end of each 'cycle' where she appears at the girls' flat and has a heartfelt one-to-one with them, each of which invariably ends with a 'Don't crush my hair!' airhug) and 'I've done everything in modelling – *everything*' critique and advice. There's nothing Tyra loves more than telling tales from the modelling trenches. Recurring favourite: informing some hick girl from Nowheresville who's battled through a photoshoot with flu, that back in her day, she managed to turn up for a shoot despite having TB, chronic stomach problems and probably a light touch of cancer and still looked totally fierce and edgy.

Learn how to be 'fierce' and 'edgy' at all times

Fierce and edgy are the most overused terms on *ANTM* – in common with much of the world of fashion, they're pretty meaningless, but a crucial endeavour to master. 'Fierce' usually just means looking furious, with your head tilted at an angle (but remember not to 'lose your neck' – a heinous crime to the *ANTM* judges). 'Edgy' is slightly harder to define, but if you manage to stick all your limbs out at improbably gawky angles, as you're balancing on ten-inch stilettos, whilst pretending to be an antelope, then you've probably nailed it.

Work out what the hell Jay is on about

Each week there's a photoshoot presided over by 'Mr Jay'. The size and colour of an oompa-loompa, but with crazily peroxided hair and all the Covergirl make-up he can grab plastered on at once, Jay is in charge of directing the shoots. By 'directing', he means making gnomic pronouncements to the girls which are in no way helpful or indicative of what they should be doing to produce a good shot.

Get in touch with your inner Girl Guide

Once you make it to the latter stages, you're carted off to foreign climes so that you can get totally lost whilst trying to get to castings in the fashion capitals of Tokyo, London, Mil-aaan, Paris and Johannesburg. It's an excuse to laugh at foreigners' accents and for Tyra to dress up in ludicrous kimonos and other bits of geographically appropriate 'costume'.

Learn how to rock a runway

Judge 'Miss J', an enormous drag queen given to sporting alarming ruffles, corsages and afros, will teach you how to clop down 'runways' like an angry horse. You'll get the knack of this by the season finale (when you will have a 'walk off' with the other semi-finalist), but will probably have to go through the ritual humiliation of 'doing a Naomi' and nearly breaking one of your Twiglet-thin ankles first.

Be a chameleon!

The best episode? The makeovers! If you have long, pageant-worthy locks you've been growing since you were ten, then say hello to your new Mia Farrow crop! Conversely, if you're currently an edgy bleached Agyness Deyn-kinda gal, you'll be awarded waist-length brunette extensions. You may, however, be the one girl who gets to keep her hair, but with added highlights/layers. The others all now hate you. Whatever: bring on the tsunami of tears.

Embrace contradiction

If living with a bunch of crazy bitches who all want to claw your eyes out isn't bad enough, you'll have to deal with the judges' weekly critiques on your performance, looks and personality. If you are 'wild' with a 'big personality' (i.e. you drink a lot and are given to inappropriate nudity), be prepared. The judges will eventually ask you to tone it down. The week after you've done so, Tyra will opine that 'the judges are wondering what's happened to the feisty girl we all loved so much? Is she disappearing in front of us? We want to see you *bring it.*' Try nodding tearfully, saying how much you want to win and working a 'smoky eye' next week. Only a fierce girl with grit can work a smoky eye.

Master walking and talking at the same time

One of the winner's prizes is the opportunity to be a Cover Girl 'spokesmodel', which in theory sounds good, but in reality means that they do awesomely bad 'My life as a Cover Girl' VTs for the subsequent series, which in the UK you don't even get to see. Trying to deliver a complicated script about mascara, whilst walking through a woodland glade and remembering the most flattering angle at which to tilt your head so as not to highlight your nose is proven, time and again by the contestants, to be tricky if not unfeasible.

Be prepared never to work as a model

The world has yet to see *any* of *ANTM*'s alumni do any actual, paid modelling outside of the show – and it's been going for ten series. Yes, despite modelling your ass off for thirteen weeks, going to castings and with the 'best' advice possible from the expert judging panel, once you've finally posed your way to the top of the *ANTM* ladder, you'll disappear back into obscurity and return home to work in a burger bar, like you did before. Except now you have a set of ratty extensions to maintain and chronic delusions of grandeur.

9

Surviving Kate Thornton:
Reclaiming Nostalgia from TV Theme Nights

In which we learn to love Freddie Starr, fondly remember Susan Stranks's hotpants, get all misty over old idents and theme tunes and settle down for a lovely bit of Christmas telly.

You might think it a little odd that within a book which mostly consists of nostalgia, there is a final chapter dedicated explicitly to it. As if you've got this far and I've suddenly said, 'And now for something about the telly.'

Sometimes the worst thing you can do to a cherished TV memory is to revisit it, as Kevin Eldon points out later. I made that mistake with *The Nightmare Man*, a BBC sci-fi horror I remember from my childhood, particularly because it was on when my family were staying in a remote chalet at the seaside and it showed a crazed monster stalking people in remote chalets at the seaside. Memories of that sheer terror have haunted me ever since. Well, until I went to see it shown at the National Film Theatre a couple of years back. Turns out it was alternately boring and unintentionally hilarious, not helped by the presence of a young Celia Imrie, who added an element of *Acorn Antiques* to the proceedings which no sci-fi horror really needs. The thing is, it was good at the time – and it really was absolutely brilliant at the time – so in a way I feel more disappointed in my desire to see it again than in its failure to stand up to a modern audience. Then again, I saw *Day of the Triffids* a week later and that was much more brilliant and terrifying than I'd remembered: even the title sequence made me sweat. That's the thing about cultural tourism, you never know what may turn up. *Fortunes of War* could be like watching a school nativity play now and *Button Moon* might stand up to *Alien* as the most convincing glimpse of extra-terrestrial life we've yet imagined; it's hard to tell.

Which is why it's important still to have hope in the future of telly rather than wallow in the past. There's so much I'd still love to see. John Humphrys on *Hole in the Wall* in a silver Lycra jumpsuit lying on his back with his legs splayed in a vertical V just before the polystyrene wall sweeps him into the pool. Al Gore on *Blankety Blank*, sitting on the bottom row between Carol Smillie and Flavia from *Strictly*, trying to recycle his cards and spoiling someone's chance to win a TV-radio-alarm clock by fucking up the Supermatch. Jeremy Irons's *Generation Game*. Godzuki joining the cast of *Emmerdale*. *Celebrity News 24*, where Chico and Maureen from *Driving School* battle it out to break news of terrorist outrages and global collapse to the nation without laughing at the silly names foreigners have.

So many programmes, so few hours on my digital recorder. Thank God. Or there'd be no time left for the most important part: slagging it off at work the next day. Because you always know, somewhere in your place of work someone is saying: 'Did you see that documentary about plastic surgery on Five last night? *My Face is a Bum*?' To which someone else will be saying that no, actually they were watching a boxed set of *The Wire*. And secretly when they hear a few of the most gruesome bits they'll be kicking themselves that they missed it.

Looking Through the Memory Window – Kevin Eldon

Ah, the golden age of television. How it's chuntered on about. As if the output of the Idiot's Lantern of yesteryear were some sort of cultural smorgasbord of quality product. Like an old lady going on about the war; it being the nation at its best where there was a real sense of community and we all loved our eggs powdered and we didn't let all that silly old death and maiming stop us having a right old knees-up.

On the other hand, with regards to modern-day television, I think it unlikely that in years to come you'll get viewers waxing lyrical about much that's on now. I can't honestly envisage anyone getting dewy-eyed about watching some sprout-faced media nonentity guffing on about Hartley Hare: *'I mean, if you think about it? He was gay? Yeah? Ooo I'm Hartley Hare! Yeah?'* Of course most of old telly probably was either dreadful or unexceptional. But there are memories, some of particular moments, some of entire programmes, that have always stayed in my brain . . .

FX: the wibbly-wobbly effects.

All boys love a good gruesome death. One that I particularly recall featured in an episode of a late sixties series called *Orlando*. The eponymous hero was played by Sam Kydd, an actor who famously appeared in about a hundred films throughout the fifties and sixties and in just about all of them he played a London taxi driver turning round and shooting out precisely one line in classic cab-ese: *'Ere y'ar guv'nor, Knightsbridge. And you're ruddy welcome to it!'* Anyway he had the lead part in this so his agent must have pulled his finger out. All I remember is he had a speedboat and some teenage companions. And they chased baddies.

One particular baddie had a death-ray in his 'lair'. Top prop for a baddie, a death-ray. I can still see the baddie's prisoner standing in a totally dark room with a spotlight shining on him from above. Baddie presses a big button and suddenly the spotlight changes colour. Sorry, goes a different shade of grey. Cue sizzling noises and screams. Smoke issues from the prisoner. A close-up of the baddie laughing like the mad bastard he is and then cut back to the victim who is now a pile of smoking ashes! Ten out of ten! Microwave executions for de yoot!

Random memories. Randy memories. Susan Stranks for example. On *Magpie* sitting in a bubble bath on an item about baths through the ages. As far as I was concerned that was one of the most achingly erotic things I had ever seen. You could see . . . her . . . bare . . . shoulders!

Oh, and what about Julia in *White Horses*! Forever cantering about in the hot Spanish sun, badly dubbed but so achingly pretty that I'd feel ill with her. This was a finer, higher thing than the confusing lust I felt for Stranks. I actually *loved* Julia.

Plenty of comedy remembrances. I adored *M*A*S*H*. Hawkeye Pearce, played by Alan Alda, was my hero. He saved lives, he got drunk, he chased pretty nurses and he was funny. So funny. I couldn't understand how anyone could be that witty. In fact that was what I wanted to be when I grew up. I wanted to be an army doctor in Korea in the 1950s out of my mind on alcohol and the sheer horror of war. Man, did that look *fun*.

And dirty old man Steptoe. I believed in his filthiness.

I reckoned I could smell the old git from where I was sitting. I loved the feeling of going eughhhh through my laughter. And then there was the highly satisfying discomfort *Top of the Pops* caused in my parents: Marc Bolan's make-up! Roy Wood's hair! Noddy Holder's voice! Everything about David Bowie!

Ah! And all these are but a tiny portion.

I know for a fact, though, that my favourite childhood television memories have become heavily flavoured by nostalgia/approaching senility. A very early Gerry Anderson puppet series was called *Supercar*. *Supercar*! It was about a super car! It could fly! It could go under the sea! I don't know if it could drive along the road or not but who cared! It had fins at the back and made a bloody great big explosion noise when its engines came on (one at a time for dramatic effect)! I'm stopping the exclamation marks now! There's a photo of me sitting in my own plastic supercar when I'm about two. My little face is beaming with chuffedness.

I recently bought the *Supercar* boxed set. I wonder if I should have. What I got was a bumper pack of medieval puppetry involving great black strings dragging big-headed freaks through slow, rather pedestrian plots. Scenery and props looked like they had been stuck together out of bog roll centres. And they probably had been. Indeed, no expense was unspared. In one episode Supercar had to fly to a jungle to get a serum from a plant because Mitch, the 'mischievous' (in retrospect 'tiresome') pet monkey of one of the characters had come over all ill. So intrepid pilot Mike Mercury and absent-minded inventor Doctor Beaker flew off and, whilst gathering the serum, encountered a wild tribe of savages. Quite apart from the extremely dodgy p.c. with regards to the natives' dialogue 'Uga wugga! Walamalama!', the tribe consisted of exactly two members. Not so much an ethnic tribe as a dodgy double act on *The Wheeltappers and Shunters Club*.

This is not to say that I didn't enjoy watching the episodes, they were still entertaining. But rather smugly giggling about something made fifty years ago on a budget of ten shillings and threepence isn't the same as sitting there immobile, smacked wordless with the sheer heart-stopping thrill of it all. I think though that from now on I'll keep all my early telly memories safely locked in the brain vault. Untarnished by an adult's perception, still illuminated by the uncritical wonder of a goggle-eyed kid.

You Are Awful . . . But I Like You: In Defence of the Guilty Pleasure – Monica Long

The notion of the Guilty Pleasure is a relatively modern phenomenon. Most frequently the phrase is used in the context of music – songs or artists we privately enjoy but publicly deride for fear of social rejection. It fuels that panic you have ten minutes before your guests arrive for dinner and you find yourself hiding Hue & Cry's 'Labours of Love' at the bottom of the CDs, with the usual, 'acceptable' suspects (Led Zeppelin, Neil Young) sitting at the top. A Guilty Pleasure is a dirty secret. Should you find yourself 'outed', or if the urge to go public overwhelms you, a solution has evolved over recent years: you can justify your admiration for late-period Phil Collins or the films of Chevy Chase, by claiming it's 'ironic'. Now, a thing can be 'so bad, it's good'. So instead of saying, 'I like this', and taking the time to explain its perhaps complex virtues, we've become lazy, and essentially cowardly, and we say 'I like this, because it's rubbish.'

Eh?

When did we stop enjoying things for their own sake? (I'm not sure exactly, but I have a feeling it was around the same time they binned the foil wrappers on KitKats, putting an end to the simple satisfaction of sliding a thumbnail down the foil crease before snapping a finger off. First they took away the trays from Bounty bars, then the foil from our KitKats. Have these people no *humanity*?) While we're on the subject, shouldn't our appreciation of a film, a song or a television show be as instinctive and sensory as our appreciation of, say, a chocolate bar? And anyway, who are these faceless hair-cuts to dictate what's cool and what's not? It's a tyranny, I tell you, a pollution, and this oil slick of irony threatens to engulf everything we've previously held to be good, clean, innocent fun.

Well, enough already. What I am about to present to you is a selection of TV shows and faces that are prime Guilty Pleasure material. They're not on HBO; chances are you won't have the box set on DVD, to be whispered about conspiratorially, in corners at parties and in work-places and then swapped amongst the 'right' friends and colleagues. They're not cool, they're not particularly clever, yet each has a quality and a charm of their own and as such, they are sources of pure entertainment for me, as the best TV should be. I've used the term Guilty Pleasure, if I'm honest, for want of a better way of setting out my list. Much like *BBC Breakfast News*, it's not quite good enough but it's there and it will have to do for now.

So, make a cup of tea, choose a suitably decadent brand of biscuits (a packet of Mint Viscounts springs to mind), have a settle and be prepared to think with your heart and not your head. I'd like to share with you some of the things that make me happy. They're not so bad, they're good. They're just good.

Catchphrase

It's not a difficult game. You don't feel a huge sense of smug self-satisfaction when you get one of the answers right. It's not a case of plunging into the depths of your brain to pluck some dimly remembered fact from your schooldays with which to wow the other people in the room watching with you. Like popping bubble wrap, or putting Hula Hoops on the top of your fingers and eating them off one by one, it's just fun! Much of the enjoyment comes from watching the contestants take Roy Walker's instructions to 'Say what you see!' quite literally. 'Dog Tears!' they shout. 'Put the Hat on the Table?' 'Is it Mouse Cooker, Roy?'

Manage to identify the catchphrase correctly and you're rewarded by Roy Walker bellowing 'Raaaiiiiiiight!' in your ear, like a man being submerged by quicksand. Obviously at the time (Saturday tea-time) the show's computer animations seemed incredibly cutting edge and if you catch a repeat on Challenge TV now, there's still a huge amount of fun to be had with the instantly recognisable sound effects. I was once on a bus when a man's mobile phone went off, and his ringtone was the Catchphrase buzzer; that unmistakable 'Beeerrdoiingggg!' sound. Whilst the rest of the bus vented their spleen at him (someone tutted), I had to restrain myself from saluting as I walked past his seat.

One of the most pleasing things about the show is its singularly British feel. There is very little sense of real jeopardy (theoretically the kiss of death for a gameshow), and even when a contestant gets it wrong, they're not made to feel bad about it. 'It's good, but it's not right,' Roy tells them. Wrong/Right, who cares! The contestants don't seem to. They've had a nice day. They got to meet Roy Walker. He was nice. A bit more red-faced in the flesh than they expected, but very nice all the same.

Dennis Waterman and *Minder*

When I was about seven years old, I thought Dennis Waterman was my uncle. As it turned out, not only was

Dennis Waterman not my uncle, but my uncle wasn't my uncle either – he was my Auntie's boyfriend, Lenny, a panel beater from Hoddesdon. I think my admiration for Dennis Waterman, which has grown over the years, has its roots in my early confusion. 'Uncle' Lenny really did look a lot like Dennis Waterman, who was a popular face in our household – and most other households in Britain – throughout the late seventies and early eighties, when *Minder* was regularly pulling in audiences of over eleven million viewers for ITV.

I've included Dennis Waterman in this list because he is the sort of British celebrity, from a certain era, who has become deeply uncool. In today's modern world of unisex skinny jeans and ironic cardigans, the idea of masculinity which Dennis Waterman represents – dressed head to toe in faded denim and looking like he smells of a combination of Lambert & Butler and petrol – seems hopelessly outdated. But it was not always thus and his tough guy roles in *Minder* and of course, *The Sweeney*, cemented his heart-throb status. Contrary to what *Little Britain* would have us believe, Waterman didn't sing the theme tune to all of the shows he featured in (though he surely missed a trick with *The Sweeney* – one of the greatest examples of TV-theme tunes-you-can-sing-the-title-to, second only of course to 'Thiiiiiiis. Is-Your Liiiiiiiiiiiiiife'), but he did a few (*Minder, On the Up, New Tricks* amongst others). To poke fun at that seems to me to be indicative of the slack and small-minded thinking behind the Guilty Pleasure phenomenon. We shouldn't be mocking Waterman, we should be celebrating his versatility as a performer and marvelling at the sheer magnificence of *I*

Should be so Good for You! Not only is this one of the greatest TV theme tunes, as far as I'm concerned, it's also one of the greatest British rock/pop songs of modern times. The rolling pub piano at the start, the chorus of geezers singing in the background: as soon as you hear it you're transported back to eighties Britain; a Britain of Ford Capris, pound notes and proper pubs. The Winchester, the members-only club which Arthur Daley used as an office and refuge from 'Er Indoors, remains one of the most memorable TV boozers. Where are The Winchesters now? Brown walls and brown carpet, red velour seating and G&Ts served in wine glasses. The only food they served was crisps and nuts, maybe pork scratchings at a push. No olives, no posh crisps seasoned with Balsamic Vinegar and Sea Salt. Wild Boar sausages and mash at £13.95? Oh my gawd, as Arthur would say. How times have changed. Channel Five recently revived *Minder* with Shane Richie. It's not quite the same, is it?

Freddie Starr

Have you noticed how difficult it is to buy a sandwich on normal, white sliced bread? It's all focaccia, ciabatta and 'wraps'. And have you noticed how many times I've referenced food in this piece which, let's not forget, is supposed to be about television? In my defence, if you think about it, the two go hand in hand. Or they do in my house anyway. But, as Ronnie Corbett would say, 'I digress' (adjusts glasses). My point is this: don't be fooled by the fancy bread. We might have all swapped our Crisp 'n' Dry for extra virgin olive oil, but make no mistake: we live in grimly pedestrian times. When the media's idea of 'dangerous' comedy is a crow-haired, stage-school dandy with a tendency to kiss and tell, it is worth remembering a TV clip from the late 1990s, when a seemingly crazed Freddie Starr threw a bucket full of maggots over Faith Brown. As this – frankly bizarre – event took place during the ITV show *An Audience With*, the weirdness was intensified by the sight of Gareth Hunt and Lorraine Chase watching on in open-mouthed horror. Now that's entertainment!

One of the reasons why I love Freddie Starr is the way his anarchic, loose-cannon act defies the tendency of the critical and cultural elite to denigrate or dismiss the 'mainstream'. His triumphant turn on *An Audience With* was typical of the unpredictable and indiscriminate nature of his comedy. Many of his greatest moments took place on Des O'Connor's sofa when, on prime-time television, Starr would gatecrash another celeb interview dressed as Adolf Hitler or, even better still, accompanied by a chimpanzee dressed as Adolf Hitler.

Starr's stocky and barrel-chested frame, used to great effect when he perfected his ape walk across the stage, seemed to just about contain the frenzied lunacy you occasionally glimpsed behind those piercing eyes – surely the craziest pair of peepers since Gene Wilder's – but just as easily, he could slip into the quiet-voiced charmer. His mightily impressive singing voice, like Les Dawson's piano playing, suggests frustrated aspirations as a 'straight' entertainer and this, along with the requisite personal battles, has predictably marked him as another entertainer stricken by 'Tears of a Clown' syndrome. But the hamster headlines unfairly detract from a unique, lunatic, and thrillingly unpredictable talent.

Climate change, terrorism, child poverty, Razorlight . . . sometimes the world can feel a very bleak place. But in even the most uncertain of times, I think we can all gain succour, maybe even joy, from the sight of a woman in white trousers who attempts – and fails – to step gingerly from decking on to a small boat.

It's not just the *Schadenfreude* or slapstick which draws me to this time, time and time again. What has secured *You've Been Framed* a special place in my heart is the show's ability to unlock subconscious memories from my past – and from our collective pasts too. Unwrapping Christmas presents in front of electric fireplaces; the idiocy of playing with a ball in a brightly lit front room; boozy afternoon barbecues in concreted back gardens; women in Su Pollard glasses dancing inappropriately at weddings; the sheer pointlessness of Swingball: *You've Been Framed* reminds us of all these things whilst simultaneously making us snort our tea through our noses. It's what Saturday tea-time telly should be all about, but it's much more than that. If you want a television programme which holds a mirror up to society, which teaches us everything we need to know about ourselves, then this is it. It shows us that life equals joy and pain. To watch it and derive pleasure from it is to accept humanity along with all its vanities and follies. Frankly, if you can't laugh while an old woman gets a ball right in the face, then I feel sorry for you, I really do.

Identity Parade – Louis Barfe

It's far too easy to blame John Birt and Margaret Thatcher for the current state of television. Although Davros's cost-of-everything-value-of-nothing extermination of the BBC improved the life of no one but himself, and the 1990 Broadcasting Act finished off just about everything else, the rot really began in the late 1980s with the demise of the regional ITV start-up sequence.

In these days of multi-channel twenty-four/seven information overload, it's easy to forget that thirty years ago, ITV made itself a mug of Horlicks and turned in for the night at about 11 p.m., bunging a droning provincial vicar on screen to make sure everyone switched off. Then, the next day, at 9.25 a.m. sharp, up came a white-on-blue list of transmitters over an extended version of your regional ITV station's ident. This piece of music, the start-up theme, was usually a jaunty march, with faint overtones of the business we call show. This mix of styles had a curious effect on some impressionable youngsters. The full two-minute version of Johnny Hawksworth's 'Salute to Thames' still makes me want to don khaki and defend Teddington Lock against any invaders, preferably with Tom O'Connor in charge of my platoon.

It was insisted on by the Independent Broadcasting Authority, then decried as a meddlesome ratbag of a regulator, now remembered fondly as the only thing that kept the barbarians in check. Not content with policing the light channel, the IBA engineering bods at Crawley Court made a weekly programme of their own to go out on Tuesdays at 9.10 a.m. As a result of Engineering Announcements, the words 'Sutton Coldfield . . .

Rumster Forest . . . Pontop Pike . . . reduced power . . . horizontally polarised' are as evocative to anoraks of a certain age as anything the shipping forecast can offer to romantic insomniacs. With Engineering Announcements shunted over to Channel 4, the fledgling TV-am closed down at 9.10, with the regions starting up again after a decent fifteen-minute interval.

Modern television executives are obsessed with branding, but can't bring themselves to admit that the old regional stations had brand identification and loyalty that the modern ITV would kill for. Before each programme, a short ident told you which member of the ITV network made it, and thus you knew what you were getting. Take the animated LWT sting, created by graphic designer Terry Griffiths and known internally as the 'River' ident, but described less officially as 'stripey toothpaste' or a 'wiggling snot college scarf'. When it came on the screen, backed by Harry Rabinowitz's faintly atonal trumpet and vibraphone fanfare, you knew you were in for entertainment. Either that or *Weekend World*. Southern had a Steve 'My Music' Race-penned tune played on Spanish guitar, signifying the imminent arrival of *Worzel Gummidge* (good), *Out of Town* with Jack Hargreaves (rubbish to a child, but rather marvellous viewed from adulthood – basically *Countryfile* shot through a reassuring haze of St Bruno smoke) or *House Party* (bleeding awful – a sort of am-dram *Loose Women*). Incidentally, I can't be the only one who supplied words to the station idents. In Southern's case, the words 'If it's Southern then it must be shite' fit perfectly.

Even now, nobody outside the industry talks about ITV1. Where I live, everyone still refers to the third channel as Anglia (logo: a silver knight on horseback revolving at 16 rpm, brandishing the company's name on a pennant to an arrangement of Handel's *Water Music*, the whole affair indicating to viewers elsewhere in the network that the following programme was either *Survival*, *Sale of the Century*, *Tales of the Unexpected*, or *Gambit*). The current crop obviously just feel jealous. They spend a fortune filming arty little sequences of women cycling down moonlit streets and sticking their ugly logos in the corner of the screen during the programmes, envious of the days when ITV franchisees could command lasting authority, large audiences and immeasurable piles of ad money with nothing more than a sheet of blue cardboard, some Letraset and a bar's-worth of Happy Shopper Segovia.

Unfortunately, having a start-up sequence relies on TV stopping, however briefly. Now, everyone in the industry believes to their very core that even a single frame of black level will have viewers reaching for the remote. If the demographic they're trying to reach consists of slack-jawed sedentary morons with overdeveloped thumbs, a thousand-yard stare and their widescreen sets adjusted to stretch everything in the wrong direction, I suppose they have a point, but what's the spending power of such viewers? TV should be a banquet with a breather between courses, not a KFC bargain bucket to be gulped without chewing or coming up for air. The magic words 'follows shortly' are foreign to television now, complete with their implication that whatever it was would be worth the wait. Maybe that's because the TV bods know that what follows now usually isn't.

Great TV Themes – Daniel Pemberton

I do hope the great TV theme is not a dying breed. It would possibly seem so in today's modern media environment. While 1960s shows like *The Prisoner* had amazing title sequences and themes that lasted almost two minutes (!), their modern equivalents, like *Lost* and *Heroes*, just have a noise that is over in five seconds. Boring. Or they just use some bland by-the-numbers rock song that really has nothing to do with the show at all. More boring.

The key, I think, to a good TV theme is first to create an interesting sound palette – use an unusual array of noises. Then write a great tune. And then try and get it played as often as possible. If you can tick all three of these boxes then you should have a classic. It's amazing we don't have more of them. A lot of TV execs like themes that sound like something else they've heard before. Or they want you to do a million different things in ten seconds leaving no space for an actual tune. Or they want it to have a 'big impact' ending. You really don't need a big impact ending – it's often the biggest false economy there is. But still they persist, making you rewrite something that was great into something that's not. I've been there – many, many times. However, every now and again someone slips one through the net and produces some gogglebox gold. Here are my personal favourites:

Grange Hill

Written in an hour by renowned TV composer Alan Hawkshaw (the only man who could not only write the themes to *Countdown* and *Channel 4 News* but also the legendary b-boy breaks tune *The Champ*), *Grange Hill* originally started life as a piece of library music called *Chicken Man* that was chucked into a recording session at the last minute. It has since become an icon of British childhood, it's bizarre funkiness instantly transporting you back to a time of Mr Bronson telling someone off and a sausage on a big fork. Wow. They foolishly changed it in the nineties to some synth tosh that no one liked. Idiots.

Knight Rider

Knight Rider. What a fucking amazing ahead-of-its-time tune. Obviously everyone else now also realises this which is why it has been sampled to death by everyone from Timbaland and Busta Rhymes to So Solid Crew and their contemporary Crazy Frog. The tune was written by Stu Phillips and the show's creator Glen A. Larson. I've always wondered whether Glen A. Larson actually did anything at all on it or whether he just wanted a slice of the action because it was his show (much like Simon Cowell and his 'songwriting' credit on *The X-Factor* theme) and thus he could do what he wanted. If anyone knows Glen A. Larson please could they find out as this one has puzzled me for years.

The South Bank Show

I agree it is not often you get to read someone citing Andrew Lloyd Webber as an influence. But his theme tune to *The South Bank Show* is awesome. Taken from his crazy classical rock mash-up album *Variations*, the theme is based on a piece by Paganini and it still sounds good today. I know it's really uncool but I do wish more people would make records like that today. I secretly love them.

The Krypton Factor

This was one of the few TV themes written by The Art Of Noise. Like much of their commissioned work (also listen to the rather patchy soundtrack of the Dan Aykroyd *Dragnet* film) it seemed to use exactly the same noises as their records of the time. Namely lots of sampled horn blasts and that 'dum dum dum' noise that was all over *Close to the Edit* and the drums from *Beatbox*. Maybe Trevor Horn had just bought some expensive new glasses and didn't want to spend any more money on memory for his Fairlight sampler. We will never know. Anyway it's one of those made-in-the-eighties tunes that has aged remarkably well. But whatever happened to the show's spooky host Gordon Burns?

Inspector Gadget

Do-do-do-do-do Inspector Gadget. Another fantastically groovy TV tune that you are probably humming to yourself right now. But did you know that the theme is pretty much a rip-off of the classical tune *In the Hall of the Mountain King* by Edvard Grieg? Work it out on the piano to see what I mean. I used to love watching the show not just for this but also for its super funky moog synthesiser underscore. I even once tried to DJ it at a night in Shoreditch many many years ago. I had previously convinced myself that this was going to be a massive dancefloor filler and send the crowd into a frenzy. It didn't. It cleared the room. Oh dear.

Treasure Hunt

Helicopters. In the 1980s helicopters seemed to be on TV all the time. Helicopters and motorcycle display teams. Where are they today? One show that used them heavily was *Treasure Hunt*. The theme tune was a super pomp synth rock monster that built to an epic crescendo. The music said, 'This could be the most exciting thing you will see on TV all year.' The show said: 'Oh look here's Kenneth Kendall and a married couple who look like they last had sex seven years ago, standing about in a room full of fake books.' What a swizz.

The Great Egg Race

I don't know how many of you remember this show but it has got one of the most killer theme tunes of all time. I tried to seek it out again researching this piece and I was shocked at how fresh it still sounded – a tight punky kinda beat with some horribly catchy Moog drops on top. It got me wanting to dance round my studio in about two seconds flat. If someone like Simian Mobile Disco sampled it up they'd have a massive hit on their hands. A gem waiting to be rediscovered.

Tour de France

Again this is a bit of a personal choice but the old theme from the Channel 4 version of this was ace. It wasn't – as many believe – Kraftwerk's track of the same name but a rather spacey sounding synth tune by some bloke who used to be in The Buzzcocks that somehow managed to incorporate French kids' tune 'Frère Jacques' *and* still sound cool.

Doctor Who

Not much more needs to be said about this. Originally written by top TV composer Ron Grainer (who also did classic themes to *The Prisoner* and *Tales of the Unexpected*), it was warped into crazy electro freakout territory by Delia Derbyshire at the BBC Radiophonic Workshop. Grainer, apparently so impressed at what the now legendary soundsmith had done with his track, offered her half the royalties. Ludicrous BBC staff guidelines, however, meant, sadly, she couldn't accept them. The current arrangement, by the normally superb composer, Murray Gold, is, in my opinion, no match for the original whatsoever. Boo hoo.

Roobarb and Custard

A viciously funky weird theme tune that sounded like a Fender Rhodes put through about six different distortion and filter pedals. In my various TV works I have tried to rip the sound off more times than you care to mention. It fitted the jaggedness of Bob Godfrey's visuals perfectly. Best not to think about the rather dodgy rave version knocked up in the nineties by the blokes from Global Communication before they were cool.

A Pitch-Black Christmas – Robin Halstead

The fairy-light programmes that once twinkled and flickered throughout the Christmas viewing season have all winked out, their now dusty bulbs never to be replaced. This isn't about your über-tinselled *My Family* special, or the now annual *Doctor Who* snow-covered spectacular, or even the risibly edited *Two Ronnies Christmas Show* compilations we're fobbed off with these days. Such shows still illuminate our screens as gaudily as an M&S ad for one of their brandy-flaming Christmas puddings. But what happened to those programmes whose sole objective was to imbue the casual mince-pie muncher with that warm and familiar festive glow?

Once upon a Yuletide, Richard Stilgoe would pop up on our screens proffering Decemberish bon mots, ably supported by some Cambridge Buskers or Kings Singers tootling out a jolly carol or six, often in Dickensian dress. Now we must settle for Brucie and Tess wishing us a cursory merry Christmas before they shuffle guiltily on to the main business: seasonally incongruous pro-am Argentine tangos. Val Doonican would be found rocking his rocking chair around the Christmas tree for many years. 'Very special guests' Pam Ayres and/or Perry Como and/or a chorus of BBC weathermen wearing scarves emblazoned with snow-cloud weather forecast symbols entertained his millions upon millions of viewers. These (Christmas) days, we're far more likely to catch an unexpectedly reborn Audrey fforbes-Hamilton threatening to divorce that lovely Richard de Vere in a bleak midwintry fashion. Bah bloody humbug.

2006 will forever be recognised as the year telly pulled

its last Christmas cracker. The following year witnessed a national disgrace. *Blue Peter* abandoned its near half-century tradition of demonstrating how to make an advent crown from twisty coat hangers and (latterly non-flammable) tinsel. As if that wasn't disappointing enough, in the final *Blue Peter* before Christmas there wasn't a single trace of the Chalk Farm Band of the Salvation Army shepherding a flock of Hark the Heralding schoolchildren into the heart of TV Centre.

Despite a bastardised 'advent decoration' returning to the show twelve months later, it was too little too late. In the 2008 Christmas edition, a children's gospel choir ding-donged half-heartedly, as if they sensed the disapproval at their presence. Just as the FA Cup was irreversibly tainted when Manchester United declined to show their rich little faces in 2000, so a part of the nation's Christmas ritual was blighted when the Man U of Sally Army bands failed to appear on the world's longest-running kids' show. Father Christmas must have been turning in his grave (the powers that be hushed up the fact that he died in 1954 in an RTA when his sleigh overturned somewhere above the A40 just outside Cheltenham).

The absence of William Booth's finest was the final nail in the coffin the schedulers buried Father Christmas in. Other final nails included the scrapping of *All-Star Record Breakers*, a decade-long excuse for key BBC talent to cross-dress long before *Children in Need* half-inched the idea; the excising of David Bowie's introduction to *The Snowman*, along with the formidable pullover his nan knitted specially for him to wear for the occasion; and the magic of not only Christmas but every single bank holiday was ruined when *Disney Time* was cancelled by a steely-eyed channel controller. Pity our poor deprived infants who will never know the simple pleasure of a celebrity of the stature of Natasha Kaplinsky or Will Young introducing clips from *The Little Mermaid*, *High School Musical* and *Candleshoe* in links pre-recorded at the Eden Project.

Britain is still desperate to cling on to any lingering traces of the ghosts of Christmas *Radio Times* past. In 2008, there was an immediate chorus of boos at the announcement that the *Top of the Pops* Christmas Day special was to be discontinued. The BBC seemed initially not to care that the Yule duty log would be overloaded with complaints but it took a predatory Simon Cowell, catching the scent of a wounded but still lucrative franchise up for grabs, to convince Auntie that it had made an error of judgement. Cowell cannot be allowed to own any more slices of Christmas. If his recent run of success continues, Cowell's *X Factor*-sponsored stranglehold over the most coveted singles chart position of the year will lead to its official branding as the 'X'-mas number one.

So might there be a fairy light at the end of the tube? After all, *TOTP* did manage to cling on to its pre-Queen's Speech slot and Noel Edmonds has somehow had his (ahem) altruistic gift-giving weepathon revived by Sky. Nolly even had the Eastbourne Band of the Salvation Army on his 2008 show. But no, such tiny lights could never add up to anything as special as some prime Rolf Harris painting a gradually emerging snowy scene on to a massive canvas. While om-pom-pomming. Festive telly really seems to have been extinguished for good.

There is only one course of action. *Doctor Who* must have a Christmas Day adventure set in TV Centre in the late 1970s/early 1980s, with Val Doonican as the villain and Dickie Stilgoe and/or Pam Ayres as his companions. And perhaps the next year the good Doctor could see fit to sort out the sorry state of the New Year's Eve schedules . . .

You Have Been Reading:

James Bainbridge is currently working on a PhD on the poet George Crabbe. He lives in Liverpool where his flat is under constant attack from the suffragettes and flappers shipped in to people the period dramas and bread commercials filming in the street outside.

Louis Barfe is the author of *Where Have All the Good Times Gone?* and *Turned Out Nice Again*. He cares far too much about the bits in between the programmes and keeps his baby daughter amused with tapes of 1980s HTV Wales continuity.

Nicola Barr is a literary agent and book reviewer. She has lived in London for almost ten years but still has a Northern Irish accent.

Andrew Benbow was initially played by a *Hong Kong Fuey* fan who eventually met Dracula with Nancy Drew. He was replaced in the nineties by an avid watcher of *Magnum* and *Quincy* repeats. The current version stays in bed eating Fruit Loops whilst watching Sid and Marty Krofft box sets.

Angus Cargill is the editor of *Hang the DJ – An Alternative Book of Music Lists*. He works in publishing as a fiction editor and so rarely watches the 'idiot box' (cf his dad) but he does have a fondness for crime shows and teen dramas, as long as they're American.

Jonathan Carter, having worked as a film journalist for various publications and radio shows, joined the BBC as a producer commissioning video content for their online cultural magazine *Collective*. Now a regular Faber contributor, he is currently working on a multimedia fiction project called *The Scurrilous Life of Mr Punch*.

Andrew Collins is a scriptwriter, author and broadcaster whose TV credits include *EastEnders, Family Affairs, Grass* and *Not Going Out*. Film Editor of the *Radio Times*, regularly heard on Radio 4 and 5 Live and seen on BBC News, he writes for *Word* magazine and records a weekly podcast with Richard Herring.

Mark Connorton lives in North London and blogged about *EastEnders* (and other TV shows) for longer than was good for his sanity. He is currently working on a novel that will not include any evil face hugging.

Sam Delaney writes for the *Guardian* and *Sunday Telegraph* and is the author of two books: 2007's *Get Smashed!* and 2009's *Night of the Living Dad*. He has presented his own documentaries for the BBC and Channel 4. He once appeared in a TV pilot as a comedy sidekick to Jerry Springer who referred to him throughout as 'Simon'.

James Donaghy has written for the *Guardian, Arena* and *Vanity Fair*. He vows not to rest until *Veronica Mars* is declared by all the greatest television show in history. He dispenses dating advice, boxing bets and television criticism at aerialtelly.co.uk

Travis Elborough is the author *The Bus We Loved: London's affair with the Routemaster* and *The Longplayer Goodbye: the Album from Vinyl to iPod and Back Again*. He hasn't owned a television set in three years

224

now but still appreciates the friendly letters – and occasional visits – he continues to receive from the licensing people.

Kevin Eldon was born in Kent years ago. He makes his living talking in stupid voices and pulling stupid faces on the television. He likes the Beatles, Buddhism and Boggle. He lives in north London with a sense of boundless optimism.

Bertie Fox was told off at an early age for gently putting his foot on the screen while audio-taping TV themes. This combination of sad obsession with a tendency to approach the telly from unusual angles might justify his inclusion in this book.

Rebecca Front is an actress and writer best known for seminal comedies including *On The Hour*, *The Day Today* and *Nighty Night* and dramas such as *Lewis* and *The Rotters Club*. She also frequently contributes to the *Guardian* and the *Independent*.

John Grindrod has been obsessed with telly from an early age. He had a letter read out concerning K9 from *Doctor Who* on *Points of View* when he was ten and appeared on *Blue Peter* the following year after breaking a world record. His digital TV recorder makes up for deficiencies in other areas of his life.

Robin Halstead is one of the minds behind spoof newspaper the *Framley Examiner* and the *Bollocks to Alton Towers* tourism guides. Aged five, he created his first fantasy TV schedule on the inside cover of an otherwise untouched colouring book.

Colin Harvey is a writer and academic. He was the winner of the first *SFX* magazine *Pulp Idol* award in 2006 and writes science fantasy stories as well as journalism and academic stuff. Colin runs the Writing Lab at London South Bank University.

Christien Haywood is like a butterfly: as soft and gentle as a sigh. His multicoloured moods of love are like his satin wings. He also enjoys tennis and golf.

Jim Helmore is the author of *Grow, Grow, Grow Monster Tomato!* and the *Stripy Horse* series of picture books. He lives in London with his illustrator partner Karen Wall. In 1981, the BBC's triffids scarred him for life.

Richard Herring is a comedian and writer best known for his collaboration with Stewart Lee in shows such as BBC2's *Fist of Fun*. More recently he wrote and starred in ITV1's *You Can Choose Your Friends* and regularly tours with stand-up shows including *Talking Cock* and *The Headmaster's Son*. His latest book *Act Your Age Not Your Shoe Size* deals with his inability to grow up.

Boyd Hilton has worked at *Heat* magazine for ten years where he is now TV and Reviews Editor. He has also written the book *Inside Little Britain* with Lucas and Walliams. Boyd has also appeared on myriad TV shows, mostly as a pundit, but did act as himself in an episode of Rob Brydon's *Annually Retentive* and authored his own Sky documentary on Britney Spears and the paparazzi. He is a regular contributor to BBC Radio 5 Live on the weekly Simon Mayo books panel.

Ian Jones is the author of *Morning Glory: A History of*

British Breakfast Television and co-wrote *TV Cream: The Ultimate Guide to 70s and 80s Pop Culture*. He contributes to the websites *TV Cream* (tv.cream.org) and *Off the Telly* (offthetelly.co.uk).

Emma Kennedy is an award-winning actress and writer. She's written loads of things for the radio and tellybox and is the author of three books: *How to Bring Up Your Parents*, *The Tent, the Bucket and Me* and *Wilma Tenderfoot and the Case of the Frozen Hearts*.

Susan Le Baigue watches a lot of telly. She particularly likes predicting the plots of *Home and Away*, especially the ones involving DNA results or psychopaths. She once appeared on *Panorama* but the TV career stalled after that.

Monica Long once saw Daley Thompson in McDonald's on Wood Green High Street. Stephanie Beacham went to her school, and she has been in a lift with Ronnie Corbett. Most recently, she saw Jonathan Pryce buying a samosa.

Daniel Maier writes for television and radio. He has contributed to a number of BAFTA- and Comedy Award-winning shows including *Harry Hill's TV Burp* and *Alistair McGowan's Big Impression* and rather more non-award-winning shows than he cares to remember.

Daniel Pemberton writes lots of music for TV. However, despite writing epic orchestral pieces and creating cutting-edge electro-acoustic works the only thing most people can remember are his 'pop pop pop' sounds you hear on *Peep Show* between scenes. Visit his website at www.danielpemberton.com

David Quantick is a script associate on *Harry Hill's TV Burp*. He has also written for *Brass Eye, Jam, The Day Today, The Fast Show* and worked with everyone from John Cleese to some bozo who does pranks on old ladies. A partly trained music journalist, he also hosted Radio 2 and 4's comedy shows *One, Broken Arts* and the *Blagger's Guide*. He loathes *EastEnders*.

Ben Rawson-Jones is a freelance journalist specialising in film and cult television, regularly writing features and reviews for the website *Digital Spy* in addition to working on his own epic screenplay. Read London-based Ben's latest rants at www.rawsonjones.blogspot.com

Adrian Riches got his square eyes growing up in a sleepy seaside town. More *Howards' Way* than *Dynasty*, he hopes one day to move back to the coast, marry 'the best boat builder in the world' and open a boutique on the marina.

Jim Shelley is the TV critic of the *Daily Mirror*. He has written for several newspapers, most regularly the *Guardian*, contributing columns such as High Anxiety and TV Dinners. His collection, *Interference: Tapehead vs. Television* was published in 2001. His hobbies include watching television and watching football. On television.

Rupert Smith is the author of several novels under various names, is a curator of gay history at The House of Homosexual Culture, and worked as a TV critic for the *Guardian* and *Radio Times* for many years.

Matthew Sweet presents *Night Waves* and *Freethinking* on BBC Radio 3. His books and TV programmes include *Inventing the Victorians, Shepperton Babylon, Silent*

Britain, *The Age of Excess*, *The Rules of Film Noir* and *A Brief History of Fun*.

Bruno Vincent is the co-author with Jon Butler of several humour books, including *Do Ants Have Arseholes?*. His first collection of gothic horror stories for children, *The Grisly Tales of Tumblewater*, is due to be released in 2010. He lives in London.

Steve Williams is a complete telly anorak who co-wrote *The Encyclopaedia of Saturday Night Telly*. He has also used his pointlessly in-depth knowledge of television esoterica to regularly contribute to the acclaimed websites tv.cream.org and offthetelly.co.uk for the past ten years.

Alex Young grew up watching telly in the 1970s, when there was nothing on except puppets and Valerie Singleton. As a child she looked quite like the girl on the test card who had the scary clown toy. She worships at the altar of both Sir David Attenborough and Tyra Banks. Her parents think her university education was clearly a waste of her time and their money.

Skip to the End: Acknowledgements

I am indebted to the many contributors for their time and ideas, and to Neil Belton, Lucie Ewin, Resham Naqvi, Jack Murphy, Darren Wall, Alex Holroyd, Julian Loose, Angus Cargill, Anna Pallai, Hannah Griffiths, Clare Yates, Kathryn Jarvis, Kate Beal, Dave Woodhouse and Neal Price for their advice and skill, the Grindrods Paul, Fern, Lily, Daisy, Ian and Tracey for their support, Joanna Ellis, Susan Holmes, Matthew De Ville, Silvia Novak and Gemma Lovett for the laughs and Lorna Rees, Conrad Westmaas, Mark Brummitt, Noel Murphy, Mark Evans and Richard de Pesando for allowing me to steal their jokes.